# Three Wodehouse Walks
## Revised Edition

Bertie Wooster's West End

The London of
Gally Threepwood and Stanley Ukridge

Valley Fields: A Wodehouse Walk in Dulwich

## by
## N.T.P. Murphy

*Edited by Elin Woodger Murphy*

### Popgood
### &
### Groolley

## Also by N.T.P. Murphy

*In Search of Blandings*

*One Man's London & One Man's London: Twenty Years On*

*A True and Faithful Account of the Amazing Adventures of The Wodehouse Society on Their Pilgrimage July 1989*

*The Reminiscences of the Hon. Galahad Threepwood*

*A Wodehouse Handbook: The World and Words of P.G. Wodehouse*

*Phrases and Notes: P.G. Wodehouse's Notebooks 1902–1905*

*The P.G. Wodehouse Miscellany*

This book is dedicated to those Wodehouseans who, over more than 20 years, have been kind enough to accompany me on these Walks and urged me to publish them.

–N.T.P. Murphy, 2009

Revised edition dedicated to the cherished memory of Norman Thomas Philip Murphy, 1933–2016.

–Elin Woodger Murphy, 2023

ISBN 979-8-218-33404-8

Published by Popgood and Groolley
Canton, Massachusetts
(https://www.facebook.com/Popgroolley)

Cover design by Jean Tillson

# *Table of Contents*

*Bertie Wooster's monogram on Piccadilly?*

# *Illustrations*

# *Foreword*

When Norman Murphy died, those who love P. G. Wodehouse's writing not only lost a friend and the most enthusiastic advocate for the enjoyment of that writing, we also lost a unique, encyclopaedic fund of knowledge that encompassed not just what Wodehouse wrote but also his life. The synthesis of that knowledge led to the publication of *In Search of Blandings*, which demonstrated the extent to which PGW used real places, people, and events to inspire the creation of the fictional world of his stories. It also led to the Wodehouse Walks, in which Norman, brimming to overflowing with enthusiasm and knowledge, took groups on walking tours of London, pointing out locations associated with Wodehouse's life and his writing, with additional gems thrown in as Norman drew on his more general delight in the history of London, something else on which he was an authority.

The lovely thing about this book is that while Norman can no longer take you on a walk in person, he is still there with you, leading the way, pointing out things of interest. And Norman's writing style is sufficiently like his speech for me to be able to hear his voice in my head, which I find quite delightful.

Norman's research and the knowledge he accrued enhance our understanding of how Wodehouse worked and add another dimension to our enjoyment of the writing. The walks he led were, and through this book still are, part of that enhancement as well as being great fun in their own right, which is as it should be in the world of Wodehouse.

I am very pleased that *Three Wodehouse Walks* is being republished and hope it will bring insight and enjoyment to another generation of Wodehouse enthusiasts.

Tim Andrew
Chairman
The P G Wodehouse Society (UK)
Chesham, June 2023

# *Introduction to the Revised Edition*

I first met Norman Murphy in March 1993, when I visited London with a friend who knew him. At that time he lived in Cumbria, but he and his wife, Charlotte, were in London because their granddaughter had been born recently. Norman kindly offered to give my friend and me a walking tour of London – and, oh, what a tour it was! We met around 10:30 am and didn't stop until 6 pm. My feet ached and my head spun for weeks afterward, such were the effects of Norman's rapid stride, machine-gun delivery, and enthusiasm for his two favourite subjects: P.G. Wodehouse and London.

Thus began a friendship that led to years of correspondence; occasional meetings at UK or US Wodehouse events; and, ultimately, marriage two years after his beloved Charlotte died in 1999. Over the subsequent fifteen years, Norman and I collaborated on many a project: he helped me with my work, and I helped him with his. In 2009 we created Popgood & Groolley in order to self-publish his books; Norman was Popgood, and I remain Groolley. After his death in 2016, I continued to publish and sell his P&G titles, and it was as I was getting low on copies of *Three Wodehouse Walks* that it occurred to me a revision was in order. Things change, after all; I already knew of at least one thing Norman had written about that was no longer where he had said it was (see Appendix 1), and surely there were more.

By this time I had moved back to the US, so the only way I could check the routes and stops was by using Google Maps/ Streetview. As I discovered the number of landmarks described in the book that are no more, I vividly recalled Norman on that first day I met him. He had not been down to London for some time, and frequently we would round a corner and come up short in front of a building site or a new modern monstrosity. "Bastards! They've done it again!" he would cry in disgust as he realized another classic Old London building had fallen to the wrecking ball.

Eventually I reached the limits of online research. At the stage when my questions could only be answered by going to the location and looking, Robert Bruce came to my rescue. He very kindly walked two of the routes for me, finding out what I needed to know and also sending pictures, some of which are included in this new edition. Additionally, he double-checked the maps I created and sent other helpful information as he came across it. After his Wodehouse map, *Blandings and Beyond*, was published (see Appendix 3), I pored through it and found a couple more sites to add to my list of Wodehouse locations not covered in Norman's walks (see Appendix 2). Thank you, Robert – you made the completion of this new edition so much easier for me.

My deepest gratitude also goes to Richard Burnip, who leads his own Wodehouse walk for London Walks. In addition to sending me old photos of The Footman building and of Berkeley Square, Richard generously looked over Appendix 2 and provided useful information on certain sites that I've used to supplement Norman's text. I highly recommend *all* his London walks (see Appendix 3).

I am extremely grateful to Neil Midkiff and Jeff Porteous, both of whom provided long-distance technical advice to this InDesign newbie. Neil also gave me much-needed assistance in navigating book publishing on Lulu.com.

Finally, my profound thanks to Jean Tillson, who designed the original cover, helped me tweak it for this edition, proofed and offered helpful suggestions for the bits I wrote, and otherwise provided a massive amount of support. She is the best of friends and the soundest egg I know.

I have added maps, a few more photos, and appendices, making this book 26 pages larger than the first edition, but it should still be small enough to carry in a large pocket or a handbag. I hope you enjoy these tours of Wodehouse's London. And here's hoping that the remaining buildings and landmarks Norman loved so well will always be there, lest we hear more "Bastards!" coming down from heaven.

Elin Woodger Murphy
November 2023

# Introduction to the Original Edition

I have read Wodehouse all my life, and as I learned more about him, I noticed that the settings of his stories mirrored events in his life. He left school and wrote school stories; he went to work in a bank and wrote Psmith in the City, a story about a young man in a bank. He went to New York as a freelance writer – and wrote stories about a young freelance writer in New York. Then I was lucky enough to read a letter in which he said that he liked using real places and houses in his stories because it saved time and trouble. He didn't have to waste time inventing fictional locations, and it also meant that he wouldn't have a character walking through a doorway on one side of the room in Chapter 5 and walking out on the other side in Chapter 13.

I perused many editions of *Kelly's London Directory*, traced Wodehouse's addresses over the years from letters he wrote, and found that nearly all his London settings were based on his own addresses or those of his family and friends. I also discovered that he liked inserting private jokes, using the address of a friend for a fictional character, knowing that only the friend and a few others would recognise the allusion.

In his 98 books I have only found about four or five 'invented' London addresses, one of which is that of Sir Jaklyn Warner in *Bachelors Anonymous* (1973). Wodehouse had not been in England for over thirty years and was unable to recall the names of the small back streets between Victoria and Chelsea he had known as a young man, so I suppose he was entitled to invent something. While he was writing *Bachelors Anonymous*, I sent him the only Pink 'Un and Pelican book he did not possess. He was delighted with it, quoted stories from it in his next two novels, and gave Sir Jaklyn an address in Murphy Mews. Probably pure coincidence, but I am very proud of it.

I conducted the first of these Wodehouse Walks in the 1980s, and since, clearly, there cannot be a Wodehouse story in every street, I began to intersperse my Wodehouse stories with anecdotes from another enthusiasm of mine, the history of London. I ask the reader's forbearance for this departure from Wodehouse scholarship, and I hope that these extraneous stories do not detract from the enjoyment of the walks.

*Norman Murphy*
*2009*

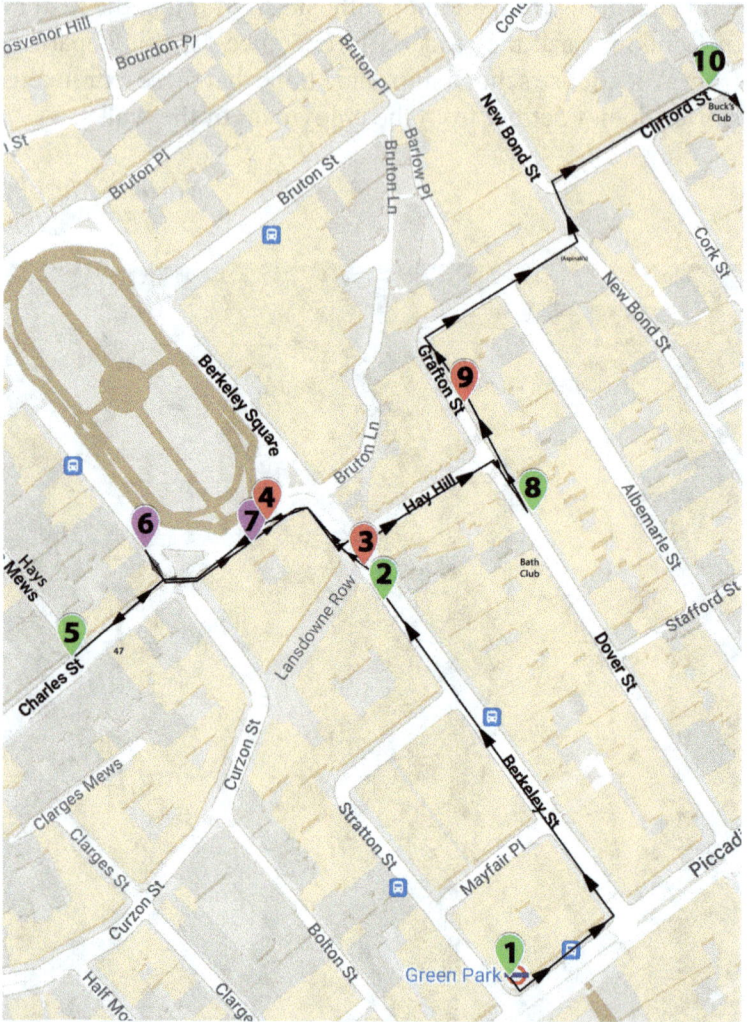

Note: All maps were created using Google Maps and Photoshop. They have been divided into sections based on what could be fitted on a page. Stops are numbered in accordance with Norman's text and are colour-coded:
- Green is a Wodehouse story.
- Red is a London story (often multiple stories).
- Purple is a London story with a Wodehouse connection.

# Walk 1

## Bertie Wooster's West End

### Introduction

This Walk looks at the London Wodehouse knew from 1919 to 1939. He and Ethel lived at several West End addresses before moving into 17 Norfolk Street (now Dunraven Street), Mayfair. It was the time when young men started wearing Homburg hats and lounge suits rather than the top hats and morning dress of their seniors. It was the era of the Drones Club, of open sports cars, reputable and disreputable nightclubs, and weekends in the country, when the craze for dancing swept the nation.

### The Walk  *(Maps pgs 6, 22, 28, 36, 48)*

**1.** *This Walk begins at Green Park Underground Station.*

I have conducted over a hundred Wodehouse Walks beginning from here since it is a convenient place at which to meet and also has a Wodehouse connection. Until 1933, this station was called Dover Street, and if you have seen the stage version of *Leave It to Psmith*, you will recall it was here that Psmith had his first meeting with Freddie Threepwood.

**2.** *Leave the station by the northern exit (north side of Piccadilly), turn left, and after about twenty yards, turn left again into Berkeley Street. Stay on the left-hand side and walk towards Berkeley Square until you see a building across the street with the number 19 beside its entrance. To the right of that is number 18.*

Wodehouse gave us two addresses for Bertie Wooster. In later books, Bertie lived in Berkeley Mansions, a block of flats that used to stand at the northwest corner of Berkeley Square (*see Appendix 2*). But his first address (see 'Sir Roderick Comes to Lunch') was 'Crichton Mansions, Berkeley Street'. I was convinced Wodehouse had a real Berkeley Street address in mind, but none of the usual sources of information – *Kelly's Directory*, electoral rolls, or the telephone directories of the period – provided any information. The problem was that, between 1919 to 1928, Wodehouse spent so much of his time travelling to and from America, his stays in London were often of short duration and in service flats.

'Crichton Mansions' was clearly a tribute to the butler in J.M. Barrie's *The Admirable Crichton* (1902), but it was years before I discovered the answer, by pure chance, when I looked up Wodehouse's application form for the Savage Club.

'Sir Roderick Comes to Lunch' came out in the *Strand* magazine in March 1922. The Savage Club candidates' book shows that Wodehouse was proposed for membership in February 1922 and gave his address as 'Ducie Mansions, 18 Berkeley Street' – the building across the road from you now. And, based on what we read in the story, Bertie's flat was probably on the third floor up there.

*Note. The original edition of this book incorrectly gave the address as 15 Berkeley Street, due to faulty handwriting in the Savage Club book. In 2013 Norman received concrete evidence that the address was actually 18 Berkeley. –EWM*

**3.** *Continue down the left-hand side of Berkeley Street. After about thirty yards, you come to Lansdowne Row on your left with some steps running down to a basement.*

Around 1780, when London was much smaller than it is now, a highwayman held up a coach here and escaped by galloping off down Lansdowne Row, which was then a narrow path. To ensure it didn't happen again, the authorities erected a gate across the lane – and it is still here. It is the graceful single bar gate tied back to the railings on the right-hand side of the steps. It must have worked because highwaymen haven't been seen around here for years.

It didn't stop the robberies, though. Some twenty years later, the Prince of Wales (later George IV) was walking back to Carlton House with two of his equerries, having spent the evening gambling at a house in Berkeley Square. They were held up at gunpoint here by a footpad, but had only a half-crown and a watch amongst the three of them. The thief relieved them of both, accompanying the action with some extremely pointed remarks on the vanity of people who spent all their money on fine clothes!

**4.** *Turn left at the end of Berkeley Street and walk along the south side of Berkeley Square, towards Charles Street, with the tall plane trees of the Square on your right.*

One of the most popular songs of the 1940s was 'A Nightingale Sang in Berkeley Square', which Vera Lynn made famous. Around 1980, someone wrote to the Press saying his parents had lived in Berkeley Square in the 1920s and there had been a bird that delighted the residents with its songs at night. He said, however, that it was not a nightingale but an ambitious blackbird!

**5.** *Continue on over the zebra crossing at the end and walk down Charles Street to the junction with Hay's Mews on your right, immediately beyond the pub 'The Footman'. On the other side of Hay's Mews, turn around so you are looking back towards Berkeley Square.*

**a.** You are now at the heart of Bertie Wooster's Mayfair. And we begin with one of Wodehouse's private jokes – Aunt Dahlia's London residence. Across the road, half-right from you, is a white building, No. 47 Charles Street. When, in *The Code of the Woosters*, Bertie was sent by Aunt Dahlia to steal Sir Watkyn Bassett's cow creamer, he realised that both Sir Watkyn Bassett and Roderick Spode knew why he had come. He promptly sent a telegram saying the job was off, addressing it to 'Mrs Travers, 47 Charles Street, Mayfair'.

Why there? Because it was the home of his friend, the author and playwright Ian Hay, with whom Wodehouse had spent over a year collaborating in writing three plays – *A Damsel in Distress*, *Baa, Baa, Black Sheep*, and *Leave It to Psmith* – and whom he knew would enjoy the joke. And for your information, Winston Churchill spent the first five years of his life in the house next door, No. 48.

**b.** Remember Halsey Court? It is the home of several young Wodehouse heroes – Jeff Miller, Jerry Shoesmith, Sam Bagshott, and Johnny Halliday – whose landlady was Ma Balsam, the softness of whose heart was equalled only by the hardness of her rock cakes.

Wodehouse had two habits which proved extremely useful in my research. When he first employed a new setting, he had the habit of either using its real name or giving accurate directions how to get there. So, in *Money in the Bank*, Jeff Miller walked west across London from Lincoln's Inn, and we read that he 'crossed Berkeley Square' and turned into the narrow entrance of 'Halsey Court'.

Look at the street sign up there on the wall in front of you – Hay's Mews. The second useful habit Wodehouse had when he invented a place name was, often, to keep the initial letter of the real name. That helped me to identify Bramley-on-Sea and Bingley-on-Sea as Bexhill-on-Sea, which Wodehouse knew because his parents moved there in the 1920s. The same thing happened here. For over a year, Wodehouse walked daily

*Sign of an earlier time*

from his house at 17 Norfolk Street (now Dunraven Street), a mile away at the other end of Mayfair – he walked everywhere – and came down Hay's Mews, or Halsey Court as he called it, to work with Ian Hay.

Wodehouse loved walking round London, and he had the gift of describing a street or location in a single sentence. He summed up this side street exactly as it was, a scruffy backwater in Mayfair, and I can confirm that, in the 1920s, the tall building up on the far right-hand side just before the corner was indeed an apartment house for single men.

Charles Street was built between 1730 and 1760 as a smart, wealthy area, as it has remained, but you will notice there are no garages along it. Obviously not, since cars hadn't been invented, but everybody round here would certainly have had their own carriage, and they were kept in small back streets like this. Look at all those small buildings on the right in Hay's Mews. The carriage and horses were kept behind those double doors, with the coachman living in the rooms above.

That was the system until the First World War. People who owned houses in Charles Street usually had another in the country, but after 1918, death duties and income tax meant many families had to give up one or the other. Often it was the London house that had to go, but many families kept their mews cottage as a pied-à-terre for the youngsters of the family who wanted to live in London. From the 1920s up to the 1960s, it was considered extremely smart – and reasonably affordable – to live in what Flanders & Swann called 'a terribly amusing mews'. These are still smart addresses, but those mews cottages will now cost you millions.

**c.** And now for the Junior Ganymede, Jeeves's famous club, named after Ganymede, the cupbearer or wine waiter of the gods. It is the building right beside you, the pub now called 'The Footman'; previously it had been 'The Running Footman', 'The Only Running Footman', and 'I Am The Only Running Footman'. When Wodehouse first refers to the Junior Ganymede, in *The Code of the Woosters*, he says the club is in Curzon Street, which runs parallel to Charles Street, but later he tells us it is around the corner from Curzon Street, which brings us back here. But we clearly want more evidence than that.

First of all, why is there a pub here at all? This is Mayfair, where the residents did not patronise public houses. As the rhyme says: 'The lower classes live / In pubs / The upper classes die / In clubs.' But when they put up these houses, the developers built these pubs as well so the servants of the houses would have somewhere local to go in the evenings. The Only Running Footman was originally built in 1749, and the building you see now is its replacement, erected in 1936. The name comes from the time when a running footman was a prestige symbol. He would deliver messages, and when you went out in your carriage, he would run ahead to make sure the toll-gates were open for you. And because there was much rivalry among aristocrats as to whose footman was fastest, this pub was, allegedly, named after a local champion who won many bets for his employer.

I got the first clue when I read a book of essays on London written by E.V. Lucas in the 1920s. One essay described 'The Club', a small pub off the southwest corner of Berkeley Square, dedicated to the use of the servants of the large houses in the area. Lucas talked to the landlord and discovered that there were strict lines of demarcation for each bar. The Private Bar was restricted to house stewards, butlers, gentlemen's personal gentlemen, and valets; the Snug Bar was for senior footmen, head grooms, and the like; footmen, grooms, and chauffeurs used the Saloon bar, while the Public Bar, at the bottom of the scale, was frequented by such untouchables as hall boys, stable boys, and Odd Job Men. And woe betide any servant who ventured into the wrong bar!

A few years later, another writer confirmed Lucas's findings and firmly identified the pub with his opening sentence: "Male attendants of the elite of Mayfair boasted their own public house, The Running Footman of Hay's Mews." How did Wodehouse know of it? He knew it because of the year he spent working with Ian Hay, who lived directly across the road and would certainly have told him of its significance.

Lord Mildmay, the steeplechase jockey and long-time friend and partner of Wodehouse's son-in-law, Peter Cazalet, lived around the corner at 46 Berkeley Square. Some years ago, I corresponded with a man who had been Lord Mildmay's footman in the 1930s, and he confirmed that The Running Footman was indeed the gathering place for the servants in the area, but he had been far too nervous ever to enter it himself. And the final proof came in 2002. Arthur Marsh, a nonagerian, told Tony Ring that he had been a footman in the house next door to the Wodehouses in Norfolk Street, and he also confirmed that this was the meeting place for the servants of the big Mayfair houses. Yes, this was the origin of the Junior Ganymede, though I'm afraid the legendary Club Book was almost certainly a Wodehouse invention.

The days when every house around here had servants to look after them are long gone, but I have the advantage over Wodehouse and Ian Hay. They would never

*The building before it became*
*I Am The Only Running Footman*
*(Photo courtesy of Richard Burnip)*

have dreamed of entering The Running Footman. That would have been appallingly bad manners; servants were entitled to their privacy as much as anybody else. But if Wodehouse had walked into the pub, I can tell you exactly what would have happened. A silence would have fallen, and nobody would have said a word until he had finished his drink and left. How do I know? Because it happened to me just a few years ago.

I'd been working at the London Library, was due to meet somebody later, and popped into a small pub off Pall Mall for a drink. I walked up to the bar and realised something was wrong. I looked round and saw the place was full of people in uniform, all looking at me politely but in complete silence. I had walked into a meeting of the stewards, waiters, and porters of the venerable clubs of Pall Mall and St James's Street. Perhaps it was the day shift coming off duty; I don't know and I didn't wait to find out. I had enough sense to say, "Gentlemen, I do apologise – please excuse me", before heading straight back to the door. It was held open for me by a man in hall porter's uniform who smiled at me benignly and murmured, "Well done, sir. Quite right" as he shut it behind me.

**6.** *Walk back to Berkeley Square, turn sharp left at the corner and stop outside the doorway of the first house on your left, No. 52. There is a fire basket attached to the railings beside the front door.*

Imagine you have just moved into this newly built house around 1735. You are having a housewarming party, and to show it is party time, you light the cresset, or fire basket, on top of the railings here. There wasn't any glass in it then; it was just a simple cage in which you lit a small fire of some sort and kept it going with judicious applications of oil or fat. You did so because London had no street lighting of any sort and a lit fire basket showed that company was expected. Rather like the balloons you see tied to front doors today for a children's party.

You can see how the fire basket was adapted over the centuries. Gas was first used for lighting in London along Pall Mall in 1807 and became popular very quickly. Hence the small pipe you can see running up the stem of the lamp. Probably around 1890 or so, electricity came in, so they altered the fire basket again with the wires coming up the gas tubing. You will see lots of fire baskets at the doorways of houses along our walk, but this one, still working, is where you can see how it developed over the centuries.

There's another reason for stopping outside this house. Although it was built between 1730 and 1740, the panelling in the front room on the first floor is nearly 700 years older.

Let's go back to 1066. William the Conqueror defeated Harold at Hastings, then took London and controlled most of Southern England. Although his army was a strong one, he knew there was much resentment at his invasion and realised some public relations work was needed. That meant getting the Church on his side, so about 1070 or so, while on a visit to Winchester, he asked the bishop if there was anything the bishop wanted and was told that a new cathedral was being built and twelve large oak trees for the roof beams would be very welcome. William agreed, and twelve large oaks were cut down and delivered to the bishop, of which eleven were used in the new cathedral roof. The twelfth tree was trimmed down to one enormous baulk of timber and put away for a rainy day in the carpenters' yard. The rainy day didn't come, and the baulk of timber sat there for a hundred years, then a hundred more and then a few more till about 1895, when a new Dean was appointed. He walked round on a tour of inspection – and tripped over the Conqueror's oak. He asked what it was and how long it had been there, then promptly ordered it to be disposed of. Everybody was absolutely horrified, but the Dean was adamant.

Then, or so the story goes, someone had a bright idea. One of the Cathedral carpenters was retiring after fifty years of faithful service, and the old question arose on what to give him as a retirement present. A gold watch? No. A presentation clock for his mantelpiece? No – give him the Conqueror's oak! What could be more appropriate for a carpenter? And so it was decided, and poor Thomas was no doubt practising his retirement speech and saying an enormous baulk of oak 700 years old was exactly what he wanted, when Mr Montague Cloete came on the scene. Who he? He was a wealthy young man on his honeymoon and had just moved into this house on Berkeley Square – and he and Thomas came to an arrangement, because that front room upstairs is panelled from floor to ceiling with the Conqueror's oak. Mrs Cloete, who lived here till after the Second World War, remembered that while Thomas did the work, they put him up in the stables behind the house and gave him tickets for the theatre every night.

And I'm delighted to say there is a Wodehouse connection. The name Montague Cloete worried me. I knew I had seen it somewhere in life's long journey, but had no idea where, and I found the answer completely by chance years later. I had occasion to look again at the accounts of the cricket matches in which Wodehouse had played for Dulwich. In 1899 he played against the MCC, whose team included – Mr Montague Cloete.

Before we leave here, have a look at the enormous plane trees which are a feature of the square. There are very few trees this size in central London because of the London fogs. Until they passed the London Clean Air Act in 1956, the coal fires everybody used meant that every couple of years, London had really bad fogs. In 1952, 4,000 Londoners died from the choking atmosphere, and the authorities realised something had to be done – so coal fires were banned in London. Conversely, the plane tree did well in smoky London because its bark absorbs the soot and the tree throws off its bark every few years. These trees have flourished since they were planted in 1789, the year of the French Revolution.

*7. Cross back over the zebra crossing and make your way back along the south side of Berkeley Square, towards Berkeley Street. Stop halfway along. (Note: There once was a large office building here, filling the south side of the square; as of 2023, it has been demolished and a new building is being erected.)*

The ground here used to be the garden of Lansdowne House (now the Lansdowne Club) over to the right, since a covenant of 1680 forbade building on this site. They didn't break the covenant till 1924, and many Londoners were outraged when the Air Ministry built an office block here. Wodehouse wasn't too happy about it, either, which is why, in *Spring Fever*, Terry Cobbold wanders through Berkeley Square and pauses to "think with regret how they had ruined this pleasant oasis with their beastly Air Ministries and blocks of flats".

Have a look at the site and try to imagine it as a grass lawn back in the nineteenth century. In 1869 Major Walter Wingfield came to dine with Lord Lansdowne and told him he had invented a new outdoor game which he was sure would become very popular. Lord Lansdowne was interested, so, the following week, Major Wingfield came out here with Lord Lansdowne, a Mr Walter Long, and a fourth young man, and drew two large ovals on the ground with white paint. He strung a net across the grass where the ovals met, and the four young men then proceeded to hit a rubber ball to and fro across the net. They soon agreed that the ovals were a silly shape, so they re-drew them as two squares. This was a great improvement, and as they had tea afterwards, they asked Major Wingfield what the game was called. He had gone back to ancient Greek and called it 'Sphairistike' (ball game), which the others reckoned was a pretty stupid name. After much discussion, the fourth young man suggested a new name which they all agreed was perfect.

The fourth young man was Arthur Balfour, who went on to become Foreign Secretary and Prime Minister. He was ennobled as Earl Balfour and died over in the northwest corner of the Square in 1930. It was during his last days that his nephew asked him of what he was most proud of having achieved in his life? Being Prime Minister? Formulating the Balfour Declaration of 1917, which led to the foundation of Israel? It is reported that his uncle said he was most proud of having coined the term 'lawn tennis' back in 1869.

And now you know where the first game of lawn tennis was played.

**8.** *Continue on towards Berkeley Street, turn right onto it, and then immediately cross over to the other side so you can turn left up Hay Hill. At the top of Hay Hill, turn right into Dover Street and walk down the left-hand side till you reach a point about ten yards before the flag over the pavement that marks Brown's Hotel.*

This is Dover Street, the home of the fictional Drones Club. It is fictional because we shall see the original Drones Club in a few minutes. So why did Wodehouse put it here? He did so for two reasons. From 1880 to 1923, the Bachelors' Club, then down at the west end of Piccadilly, was the club most favoured by young men about town. Wodehouse mentioned it often in his early stories, but in *Jill the Reckless* the plot required Freddie Rooke to meet his friend Algy Martin in another young man's club. So Wodehouse simply invented the Drones Club as a fictional alternative to the Bachelors'. The same thing happened in *Leave It to Psmith* when Freddie Threepwood had to be a stranger to Psmith, so Wodehouse again used the imaginary Drones Club and put it in Dover Street.

Wodehouse chose Dover Street for a practical reason. Piccadilly, Pall Mall, and St James's Street possessed so many famous clubs already that a new one would stick out like a sore thumb, but Dover Street was another matter. Piccadilly lies about 150 yards down the road ahead of you. Between 1910 and 1930, Dover Street was home to at least fourteen clubs; most seem to have had a life of five years or less. To emphasise the point, the large building on the corner of Hay Hill and Grafton Street behind you was, in a period of twenty years, home to the Turf Club, the Berkeley Club, the Empire Club, the Royal Navy Club, Arts & Letters, the Junior Conservative, and the British Motor Boat Club. No wonder Wodehouse was able to slip another club in here.

But one Dover Street club did provide an important element of the Drones. We all remember that Bertie Wooster had had it in for Tuppy Glossop ever since the occasion Tuppy bet him he couldn't swing down the club swimming pool by the ropes and rings, and then pulled back the last ring so Bertie had to drop into the water in his dress clothes. And that can only be the Bath Club, which used to be at No. 34 on the other side of the road (the new building opposite the Brown's Hotel entrance). It went up in flames during the war in 1941, and the club had to move elsewhere.

Wodehouse would have known of the club, founded by Lord Desborough in 1894, since two of his uncles were members. Lord Desborough – mountaineer, athlete, and big game hunter – was one of those people who was never happy unless engaged in such strenuous activity as swimming under Niagara Falls – twice – or winning a silver medal fencing for his country at the age of 41. He wanted somewhere in London where he could swim, so he and a few friends bought the house and installed a swimming pool on the ground floor with gymnasium ropes and rings above it. Apparently the routine was to change into swimming costume, do some strenuous and exhausting exercises on the ropes and rings, then drop in the water, swim your fifty lengths or whatever it was, have a shower, and join your friends in the bar.

My problem was that the Bath Club was a highly respectable London club, and the likelihood of the members playing silly tricks on each other as Tuppy played on Bertie seemed highly improbable. How did I find out, especially when the club had been destroyed in 1941? You couldn't just go around London in the 1980s asking complete strangers if they had been members of a club that had been destroyed forty years before.

My luck changed in 1995 when I was in the Savage Club standing beside two elderly gentlemen at the bar, and I heard one of them say, "I still miss the old Bath Club, you know." The thirst for information overcame my good manners and I rudely interrupted them, apologised, and started asking questions. Yes, he had been a member of the Bath before the war. Yes, there had been ropes and rings over the swimming pool on which members exercised before they swam. Yes, members did swing down the pool by the ropes and rings with their clothes on. It happened all the time.

I remember pausing before I asked the last, vital question. Did it ever happen that a member bet he could swing down by the ropes and rings and then somebody pulled back the last rope so he fell into the water with his clothes on? I have never forgotten the way his face changed. "Yes, that happened often as well. The bastards got me once!"

With tremendous self-control, I managed to restrain my exultation at finding another legend had become fact, and asked what had happened. It is a sad story. It was about 1938, and he had just been admitted as a member of the Bar. His parents had bought him his first Savile Row suit to celebrate the occasion, and his 'friends' in the Bath Club had given him a celebratory lunch, after which they had plied him with port. They then issued the challenge to swing down the pool, saw him well on his way, then pulled back the last rope. He added, bitterly, "The thing was, the swine pulled back the first one as well so I couldn't go back." And he had had to drop into the pool in his new suit.

In order to ease the strain of what was clearly still a very bitter memory, I introduced myself properly, discovered that my new acquaintance had been a member of the Bench, Judge Richard Vick, and asked why he had joined the Bath Club, which got me my second bonus. Was the Bath particularly popular with barristers then? No, it was simply a very convenient club to join. I was puzzled by the word 'convenient', so he explained: "If you saw someone in Berkeley Street you didn't want to meet, you could nip in the back door of the Bath, walk through to Dover Street, cross the road into Brown's Hotel, walk through that, and you were in Albemarle Street."

I found this puzzling. This was a retired judge I was talking to, and you can't get more respectable than that. Who were these mysterious people he was trying to avoid? From this pillar of the community came words which could have come straight from the lips of Bingo Little or Freddie Widgeon: "Oh, you know, the usual people. Policemen, girls, girls' mothers, people like that!" He never came to the Savage again and died some six months later, but he should be remembered kindly by all Wodehouseans as the man who confirmed that Bertie's ordeal was based on fact, not fiction.

Before we leave Dover Street, a quick word on Brown's Hotel, the oldest in London. It was opened by James Brown in 1837, whose wife had been lady's maid to Lord Byron's wife. The hotel flourished, and in 1876 Alexander Graham Bell was a guest. Bell demonstrated his latest invention with the first telephone call made in England from the hotel to a Mr Henry Ford (not him, another one). Teddy Roosevelt, later president of the United States, was married from here in 1886, and Franklin D. Roosevelt continued the family tradition by spending his honeymoon here in 1905.

**9.** *Turn back the way you have come and walk along Dover St, which becomes Grafton Street at the corner with Hay Hill.*

About twenty yards along Grafton Street is a plaque on the wall the other side of the road, commemorating Lord Brougham, who once lived here. He was the brilliant lawyer who became Lord Chancellor, had a form of coach named after him, and made the south of France a fashionable winter holiday spot for wealthy Britons; that is why there is a statue to him at Cannes. But he is best remembered today for the caricature of him on the cover of *Punch* that remained unchanged for nearly a century. He was the character being pulled in a coach at the bottom of the picture.

On the wall above the plaque is a small shield, showing a red cross with a dagger in the left-hand corner. When this part of London was being developed in the eighteenth century, the City of London was worried about the loss of the small rivers that provided the City with much of its water. In order to keep some control over the situation, they bought various plots of land outside the city boundaries in the West End, and this house used to overlook the stream running down Hay Hill. The badge shows that the householder pays taxes to the City of London, not Westminster.

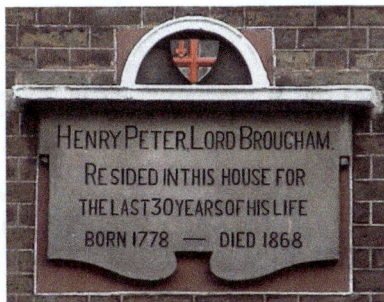

**10.** *Follow Grafton Street round to the right and make your way down to New Bond Street at the end. The last building on your right is the former location of Asprey's the jeweller, who were here in Bond Street from 1847 to 2021. Asprey's (now located in Bruton Street) was the origin of Aspinall's of Bond Street, the jeweller patronised by Bertie Wooster.*

*Turn left at the statues of Churchill and Roosevelt on the bench, then directly right into Clifford Street. Walk along the left-hand side and stop just before the junction with Old Burlington Street on the right. Across the road from you is an eighteenth-century building on the corner: 18 Clifford Street.*

Surprisingly, there is only one accurate description of the Drones and, it is to be found on the frontispiece of *Eggs, Beans and Crumpets*: "In the middle of London's Mayfair, there is a dark sombre building known to taxi drivers and those who frequent it as the Drones Club." A pretty good description for that building across the road because this is Buck's Club, the major source of the Drones.

Before we look at the detail, let us assume that you and your friends start a club. It is popular, more people join, and everybody enjoys it, but over the years, you and your friends

21

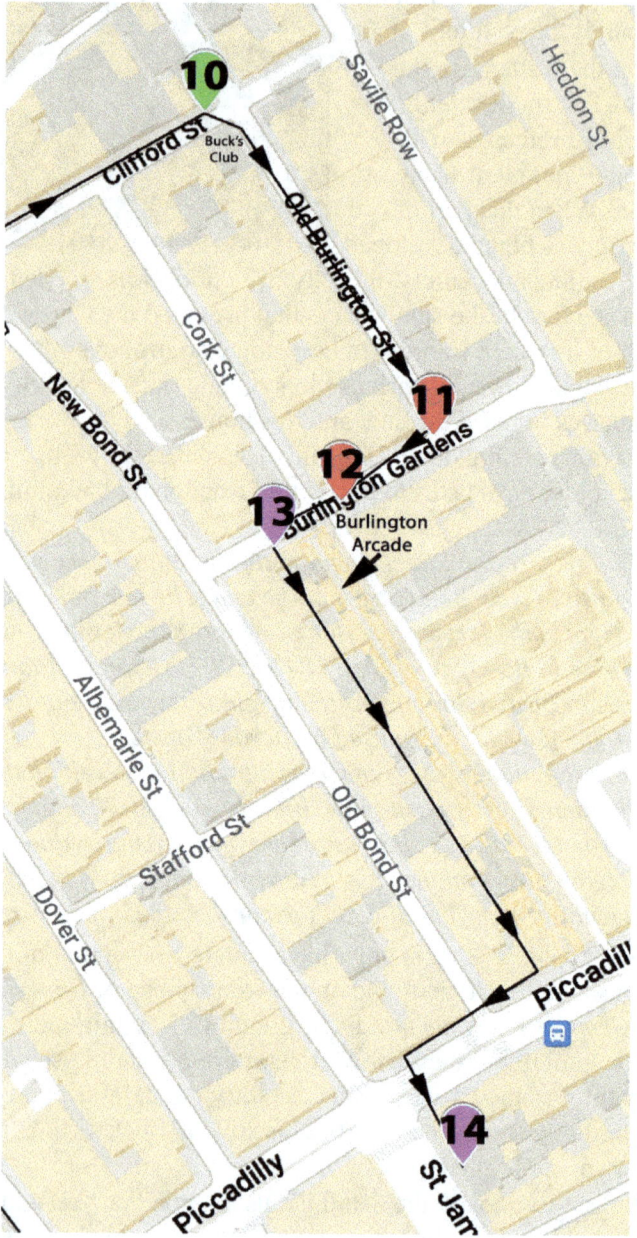

get older, more set in your ways, and then youngsters don't want to join anymore. That is what happened here. Founded in the 1880s, the Bachelors' Club was very popular, but its membership grew older and young men found it boring. In 1917 Captain Maurice Buckmaster was serving in France, and he and a few friends resolved that, if they survived the carnage, they would found a new London club for young men. Buckmaster did so in 1919, and Buck's Club has been here ever since.

That is why, in the early Wodehouse stories, it is always the Bachelors' that is mentioned. But in *The Inimitable Jeeves*, when Bingo Little is telling Bertie Wooster of his great love for Honoria Glossop, he does so in Buck's Club because Wodehouse knew that Buck's had now superseded the Bachelors' as the popular club for young men. He used the real name a few times in his stories but realised that could lead to complications, so he remembered his fictional alternative to the Bachelors' and called it the Drones.

How can I be so sure it was this club? In that first mention in *The Inimitable Jeeves*, Wodehouse gave us two clues, though both took me some time to confirm. Bertie wished Bingo would lower his voice a little because, as Bertie says: "Fred Thompson and one or two other fellows had come in, and McGarry, the chappie behind the bar, was listening with his ears flapping." McGarry, you might recall, was the Drones barman who could tell the weight of anything, including fat uncles, just by looking at it. I do not know how true that is, but I can tell you that McGarry was the name of the barman here from 1919 till 1941.

Fred Thompson, the other name Bertie mentioned, took longer. I realised at once that the name did not have what I call 'the Wodehouse rhythm'; the 'sound' was wrong. When you read a name in Wodehouse that doesn't sound 'right', then it is usually a real one. (Fred Patzel, the hog-caller, was another one.) It was months before I remembered who Fred Thompson was. He was a friend of Wodehouse's, an early member of Buck's who worked on many successful shows with Guy Bolton, co-wrote the book of *The Golden Moth* with Wodehouse in 1921, and is mentioned in *Bring On the Girls*. Bertie's mention of him coming into the bar is another of Wodehouse's private jokes, a reference that he knew Thompson would appreciate.

We read often of the Drones Club weekends at Le Touquet. In the 1930s, the Buck's Club's weekends in Le Touquet were a well-known event, and Wodehouse used them to set the scene for the incident that caused all the trouble in *Uncle Fred in the Springtime*. You will recall that Mustard Pott was shadowing Valerie Twistleton at Le Touquet and was grabbed outside a house by the golf course. While Wodehouse was writing that book, he was delighted that his daughter Leonora and her husband, a member of Buck's, and two other friends, also from Buck's, stayed with him for the Buck's Club weekend – in his house beside the golf course.

I was allowed access to the Club Members' book; Wodehouse was never a member, but Guy Bolton joined in 1933, and he was Wodehouse's closest friend for over sixty years. Further, I have seen at least three notes from Wodehouse to Bolton accepting invitations to lunch at Buck's Club. That is how he knew the club so well.

Towards the end of his life, Wodehouse was asked if the Drones was based on Buck's. He was surprised by the question. He had not realised that what was common knowledge in London in the 1930s had become legend by the 1970s. He confirmed that Buck's was the main source but specifically mentioned the Bath Club in Dover Street as being the source of Bertie's humiliation at the hands of Tuppy Glossop.

In case you are wondering, Buck's Club are fully aware of their fictional counterpart. They were kind enough to ask me to tell them all about it at a dinner where, confirming

Bertie Wooster's comment on what a small world it is, I was seated beside a peer who was the grandson of a man to whom I devoted six pages in *The Reminiscences of Galahad Threepwood*.

**11.** *Cross over the road and then proceed to walk down Old Burlington Street. Pause at the end of the street.*

The large building in front of you is the back of Burlington House, the home of the Royal Academy. It is named after the Earl of Burlington, who moved here in 1668. Our next story revolves around a later resident, Lord George Cavendish, who moved here in 1815. He liked the house but found there was one slight problem. Alongside his garden was a footpath running down to Piccadilly, and people kept throwing things over the hedge into his garden. Lord George built a wall along the path, but things were still thrown over it – dead cats, empty bottles, things like that. So he built the wall a bit higher. Stuff still came over, so he raised the height again, and again, and a fifth time. It seemed to have become a battle between him and London's vandals, and after the fifth addition, he must have done some lateral thinking. He could only stop rubbish coming over his wall by preventing it being thrown up on the other side – so he built the Burlington Arcade.

**12.** *Cross the street, turn right, and walk along Burlington Gardens towards the entrance of the Burlington Arcade. Just before you reach it, there is a large gateway on your left with a roadway running away from you and an immensely high wall on the right. Pause here.*

If you look along the line of the wall carefully, you can see the building lines where Lord George built the first section about six feet high, the next about ten foot high, and the lines of the three higher layers can be traced running away from you.

One more story before we walk down the Arcade itself. The Arcade immediately became a very smart shopping spot, and it was decided to have beadles to keep order here. They have powers similar to ushers in court, and you will probably see one as you walk down the Arcade. They wear a top hat,

25

and their uniform is blue and grey from the colours of the 10th Hussars, because that was the regiment of Lord Chesham, who bought the Arcade from Lord George Cavendish and started the beadle system here.

The rules laid down in 1819, when the Arcade was opened, included a prohibition on singing or whistling in the Arcade, running, carrying parcels (only servants carried parcels in those days), and various other rules, including a ban on wearing swords. This was to prevent people fighting impromptu duels here. When I wrote *One Man's London* (1989), I came here to check my facts with the senior beadle. He confirmed that parcels are now permitted, but singing, whistling, and running are still banned. And then I asked about wearing swords.

As soon as I did so, his face changed. There was a story here, but he was reluctant to tell it. All the beadles were then ex-warrant officers (sergeant majors), and luckily I recognised the medal ribbons on his coat, wore one of them myself, so I felt bold enough to say, "Come on, sar'nt major. What happened?" – and it worked.

In 1982 we fought the successful war in the Falkland Islands, and a senior naval officer was properly rewarded with a decoration by the Queen. He went to the Palace to collect it and, being a good husband, decided to buy a piece of jewellery for his wife. He was, of course, in full dress uniform – which included wearing a sword – and the Arcade knew he was coming! He arrived at the Arcade in a taxi, got out, and found himself facing the senior beadle: "Sorry, sir. No swords inside the Burlington Arcade!" He was furious but the beadle was adamant, so the admiral had to take off his sword and thrust it at an astonished taxi driver before he was allowed in.

So, don't wear your sword in the Burlington Arcade!

*Note: From here to the end of Walk 1, there are fewer Wodehouse sites and references and more of a focus on London. Keep going if you are enjoying Norman's London stories, but for a more Wodehouse-rich route, turn off here, or at the end of the Burlington Arcade, to switch over to the second walk. See Appendix 1 for directions and a map.*

**13.** *Have a browse in the Arcade as you proceed down towards Piccadilly. There used to be, on the left, a window full of silver figures of animals. Imagine it is still here as we consider silver cow creamers.*

When you see a window full of silver stags, horses, and foxes, it usually means the silver is Victorian. Despite what one hears about the Victorian class system, they encouraged entrepreneurial success and many men did rise from a workbench to become millionaires. In those days, if you had money you flaunted it and the New Money bought stately homes, grouse moors, and all the rest of it and covered their dining tables with sporting silver figures. Around 1870 it became a point of pride to have so much silver on the table that the tablecloth itself was nearly invisible.

The cow creamer Bertie's Uncle Tom coveted was a different matter. They were eighteenth-century, and the story is that their popularity began with the Duchess of Richmond around 1740. She was the leader of fashion at the time, and George II was so struck by her riding costume of dark blue trimmed with white stripe that he adopted it as the uniform of the Royal Navy. Apparently that unlikely anecdote has a good historical basis. The legend is that, around 1740, the Duchess decided that drinking a cup of tea should be more of a social occasion, and she led the way by having an elaborate silver tea service made. Society followed her lead, and John Schuppe, a Huguenot silversmith working in London, saw his chance. In the 1750s, he started producing his silver cow creamers, and they became immensely fashionable. There are some in the Victoria and Albert Museum today.

To find out more, I went to Bentley's in Bond Street, and they were delighted to tell me all about them. They kindly showed me the Schuppe cow creamer they had in stock and agreed it was completely impractical since the interior is full of rough, jagged edges where milk would collect and be impossible to clean. They also agreed that cow creamers have joined Toby jugs and horse brasses as useless objects people just like collecting. When I went to see them, their Schuppe cost £15,000, though a modern version can be bought for £500.

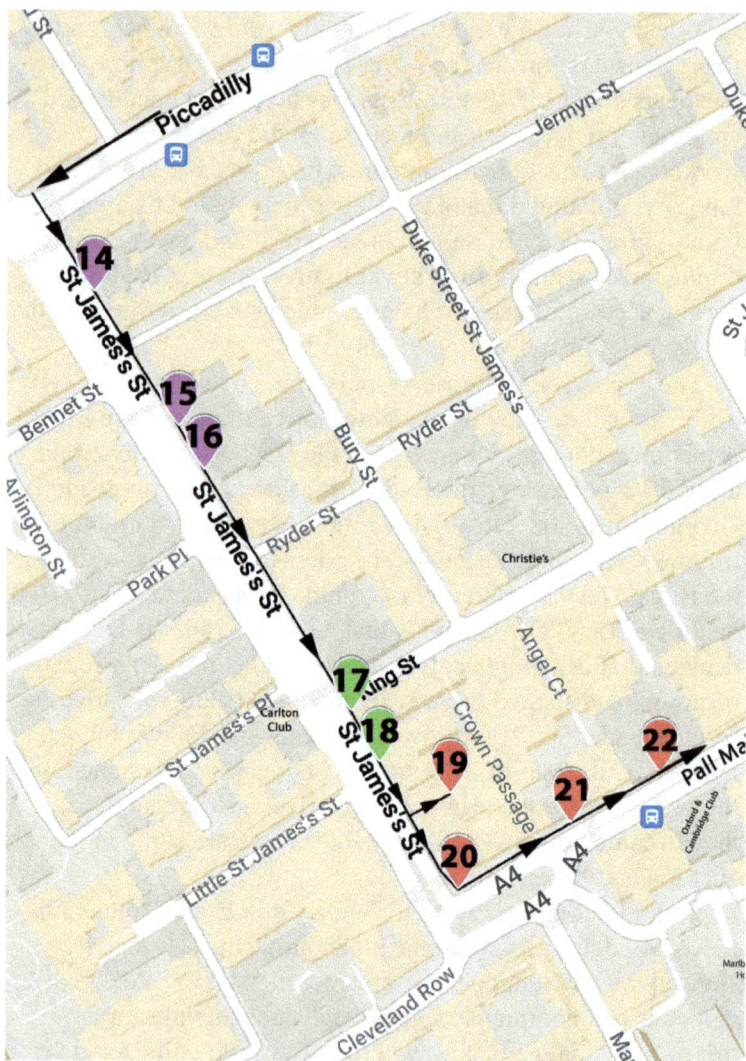

Just as I was leaving, I remembered Aunt Dahlia's comment on cow creamers that were 'modern Dutch'. The Bentley's chap was puzzled by this until I explained the comment had been made in the 1930s. His face cleared, and he said Aunt Dahlia was right. Around 1890, Dutch silversmiths began to make replicas of the Schuppe creamer, and as the shopkeeper in Bertie's narrative told us, people soon learned you had to check the hallmark. And, if you are wondering if Wodehouse had a real shop in mind, then the directions Bertie was given to the antique silver establishment just 'beyond the Oratory' will take you to James Hardy's antique silver shop at 235 Brompton Road, where they have been since 1853.

*Another Arcade-based story from Norman – a personal one – has been moved to Appendix 1; see page 99.*

**14.** *Continue down the Arcade to the entrance on Piccadilly, turn right, go down to the traffic lights, and cross Piccadilly. Turn right again and then left down St James's Street. Stop just a few yards down on the left beside an eighteenth-century building with a bow window to the left of the doorway.*

We are now in St James's Street, one of London's great club streets, though there are far fewer clubs here now. The days when club servants were happy with wages of a pound a week are long gone, and this, together with the increase in rents, has reduced the number of clubs on this street from twelve to the present five. The beautiful building beside us now is White's, London's oldest club, founded in 1693. Beau Brummel was a member here; he was the leader of fashion in Regency London and possessed an astonishing degree of arrogance. When someone asked him to repay a loan, he replied, "I've repaid you twice. I let you take my arm for fifty yards along Piccadilly and I've nodded at you from the bow window of White's. What more do you want?"

This cavalier approach to money worked well so long as shopkeepers knew that Brummel enjoyed the close friendship of the Prince Regent (later George IV), but Brummel's arrogance led to his ruining that relationship as well. One morning in 1816, down at the end of this street, Brummel met Lord Alvanley walking with the Prince Regent, who was grossly overweight and very sensitive about it. Brummel's greeting – "Morning, Alvanley! Who's your fat friend?" – meant that Brummel immediately became a Society outcast. He was soon declared bankrupt and had to leave the country. (And if the remark sounds vaguely familiar, it is because Wodehouse used it in *Something Fishy* when Mortimer Bayliss asks Bill Hollister: "And who is your stuffed friend?")

Wodehouse did refer to White's Club once, though he changed its name. In *Uneasy Money*, we learn that Lord Dawlish is secretary of what is clearly a very senior London club. Remember the name? It was Brown's, not White's.

**15.** *Continue down St James's Street till you reach Dr Harris & Co., the chemist on your left.*

Harris's is an appropriate place to speak of Jeeves's hangover cure. I don't know about you, but the aspect of it I always remembered was that it made your eyeballs leap from their sockets. Wodehouse referred three times to the chemist "at the top of the Haymarket", which my researches show were Heppell & Co, but they vanished long ago. However, some years ago I read in the papers that White's Club and Boodle's Club had had big dinners the night before, and (I quote) "there had been a heavy run on Harris's hangover cure".

As soon as I could, I called in at Harris's. The conversation went as follows:

"Good morning. Before you show it to me, could I ask some questions about your hangover cure?"

"Certainly, sir. What would you like to know about it?"

"Well, firstly, is it dark brown and sinister in appearance?"

"Yes, it is."

"Oh! Well, secondly, does it taste revolting?"

"Yes, it does indeed."

"Thirdly, forgive me asking this, but I do have a reason. Does it make your eyes pop out?"

"Yes."

"What! Really? How does it do that?"

"It's the ammonia we put in it!"

It is with much sadness that I have to say, because of some footling legislation, Harris's have since ceased producing their elixir.

**16.** *Move to the building immediately beyond Harris's.*

This gracious building beside you is Boodle's, a gentlemen's club founded in 1752. Brooks's club, just a few years younger, is across the road. You will remember that a common topic in Wodehouse is the plight of owners of country houses whose great-grandfathers had gambled away the family fortunes with charm and grace at the gaming table. Wodehouse usually gave these gambling ancestors the prefix 'Beau', thus firmly locating them in the late eighteenth century. He wasn't exaggerating. I think it was at White's around 1790 that about £3,000 pounds (nearly half a million quid today) was wagered on which raindrop would reach the bottom of the window first. Another similar incident occurred either here or at White's when a passer-by collapsed in the club doorway. The members gathered round, and a book was opened: would he live or would he die? After ten minutes or so, somebody suggested a doctor be called. This was considered an outrageous suggestion: "Call a doctor? We'll have no foul play here. Let him take his chance!"

Well, that was all a long time ago, but I'm delighted to tell you the tradition is not quite dead. In 1954 a member of Boodle's took a bet he could hit a golf ball from the steps of St Paul's and get it through the club doorway here in under a thousand strokes. He did it in just under 300.

And I recall that when the Frisbee became popular in the early 1960s, a member of White's made a bet that he could skim a club saucer through the windows of the Devonshire Club across the road. At least one broken window showed it could be done. I find that very reassuring, don't you?

Incidentally, if the names Brooks's and Boodle's strike a vague chord in your mind, it is because, as with Halsey Court, Wodehouse kept the initial letter of the real name. Bertie Wooster told us his Uncle George belonged to two clubs in St James's Street. They were the Buffers and the Senior Buffers.

**17.** *Continue down the left-hand side of St James's Street to King Street. Cross over, then look down King Street.*

If King Street, St James's, sounds familiar, it is because Freddie Threepwood took a service flat here in 'Lord Emsworth Acts for the Best', and Gally Threepwood had a flat here in *Full Moon*. Which flat did they live in? See the red flag marking Christie's auction house down on the left-hand side? See the balcony above it? That is the service flat Wodehouse and Ethel took in December 1921, another example of Wodehouse using one of his own London addresses (11 King Street, St James's; *see also note in Appendix 2*).

Across St James's Street from you now is a stucco building with a balustrade at the top. See it? That is the Carlton Club, whose clubhouse in Pall Mall was bombed during the war, so they moved here into the old Arthur's Club building.

Having said that, let us consider the foul manners of Wodehouse's Duke of Dunstable. You will recall that, if he thinks he is being thwarted, he will throw eggs at you or break up your furniture with a poker. Was there ever a member of the old aristocracy as boorish and arrogant as that? I regret to say there was. In the later years of Victoria's reign, the Earl of Euston, a member of the Carlton Club, decided a waiter was thwarting him, so he threw him out the window onto the pavement below. He made no apology and met his fellow members' horrified reproaches with the simple words: "Put him on my bill."

**18.** *Proceed on down St James's Street till you come to Lock & Co., London's oldest hatter, on your left.*

Do you remember Jno. Bodmin of Vigo Street, the hatmaker par excellence of 'The Amazing Hat Mystery'? Why Wodehouse put him in Vigo Street, I have no idea because there has never been a hatter in Vigo Street and there has never been a hatter called Jno. Bodmin, either. Because Lock & Co. are London's oldest hatters and have been making hats for royalty, the nobility, and gentry since 1676,

I nominate Lock's as the most likely origin of Bodmin's. Lock's made hats for Nelson, Wellington, and Queen Victoria and have held the Royal Warrant for centuries. I celebrated my promotion to lieutenant-colonel by coming here to buy a bowler, though Lock's will invoice you for a 'Coke', not a bowler. This is because they made the first bowlers here for William Coke, who came in one day in 1850 and said he wanted a strong, round hat for the gamekeepers on his Norfolk estate. I can confirm that the gamekeepers on the estate still wear them. But even Lock's had to modernise, and there was consternation amongst its clientele when they started selling women's hats some years ago.

If you peer through the left-hand window, you can see the hats they made for Wellington's officers in the Napoleonic Wars on the shelf high up on the wall.

I have learned that Wodehouse bought a new top hat for Leonora's wedding, and I suspect there may have been a problem over its delivery. Leonora was married in December 1932; 'The Amazing Hat Mystery' was written a matter of weeks later.

**19.** *A few yards further on, turn left into the narrow alley, Pickering Place, noting the historic Texas Embassy plaque at the entrance, and walk along to the courtyard at the end.*

There has been argument over the origins of Pickering Place, but the earliest maps of the street are clear on the matter. When Henry VIII lived in nearby St James's Palace, there were hundreds of courtiers and servants to be fed, and the court needed a constant supply of such staples as hay, straw, meat, and milk. You have just walked through the narrow passage which early maps show was the entrance to Henry VIII's cowshed. Many historians claim it was a royal tennis court, though I dispute this since it is too small. Whichever it was, this narrow passage certainly dates from Henry's time.

Pickering Place became notorious as London's last duelling ground, which raises another historical facet I have always enjoyed – how a social habit could die because of a single incident. Consider duelling. The story goes that in 1772 Richard Sheridan, the playwright, fell in love with a Miss Linley, and another admirer, Major Matthews, challenged him to a duel. They began the fight with swords in Hyde Park, but a large crowd gathered, and they were forced to stop and adjourn to a tavern yard in Piccadilly, where they began all over again. Unfortunately, the crowd followed them, and they adjourned again to another pub in Covent Garden and carried on fighting there. I don't know how long it went on, but eventually both of them were so exhausted that they stopped by mutual consent. Since neither was much good at duelling, they weren't hurt, though they were both covered in blood and their clothes were in ribbons.

Now, this was in 1772, when elegance was all. Society immediately decided that swordplay was a messy business not to be pursued and promptly took up duelling with pistols. Far more elegant. Joseph Manton, the finest pistol maker in England, always said he owed his success to Mr Sheridan's clumsiness with a sword.

Note the windows in the building on your right. These buildings were put up in the 1730s and the rough, dimpled glass in the windows might well date from then. It certainly precedes today's plate glass by a hundred years or so.

Resting against the railings at one side is a plaque with a man's head on it. It has been there since about 1956 or so, when I saw workmen take it down from the bomb-damaged wall of what is now a restaurant on the northern side and place it here – as 'a temporary measure'! It commemorates Lord Palmerston, who was twice Prime Minister in the 1850s. His prospects looked very dodgy before his second term of office but he got in, and he attracted popular admiration when he was cited in a divorce case at the age of 79.

As you go back along the passage, look at the half-timbered walls above the wooden panelling. That isn't brick up there; it is just clay, straw, and mud, anything that would harden enough to keep the rain out, but it needed timber framing to give it stability. Until well into the sixteenth century, bricks cost a lot of money, and people would not waste money on a small, unimportant passageway like this. And the reason bricks cost so much is that, when the Romans left around AD 410, we stopped making bricks in this country and didn't make any more for nearly a thousand years. We'd forgotten how! We just got by with stone, flint, timber, and wattle and daub, which is what this probably is.

**20.** *Go back to St James's Street and turn left down to the corner. Before turning left along Pall Mall, pause to look at St James's Palace, across the street.*

This is St James's Palace, which Henry VIII re-built after grabbing it from the nuns of the convent of St James. If there is a Guardsman on sentry duty over there, there is a simple method of working out which regiment he is from. If the buttons on his tunic are in ones, he is in the Grenadier Guards; if in twos, he is in the Coldstream Guards. Buttons in threes mean the Scots Guards; in fours mean the Irish Guards; and sets of five mean the Welsh Guards.

Do you remember how Monty Bodkin realised he had made a bad mistake when he had 'Sue', for Sue Brown, tattooed on his chest? The same thing happened here. Carried away by his passion for Ann Boleyn, Henry VIII had the initials H and A placed on the other side of that gateway as well as being carved on stone fireplaces inside. Not a good idea when there are four more wives to come – so be careful with those tattoos.

**21.** *Walk along Pall Mall about 20 yards until you are opposite the gates running down to St James's Park. Left of the gates, you will see a red-brick building set well back from the road.*

That building is Marlborough House, built for the Duke of Marlborough early in the eighteenth century. His wife was a very strong-minded lady, and when she found the architect, Sir Christopher Wren, was being cheated by the building contractor, she sacked him and supervised its construction herself. It was she who had the bright idea of importing cheap Dutch bricks to build the house, and she saved even more money by bringing them over from the Continent as ballast in Navy ships. She terrified everybody who came into contact with her, including George I. When he moved into St James's Palace in 1714, she just ignored him, referring to him as "my Hanoverian neighbour".

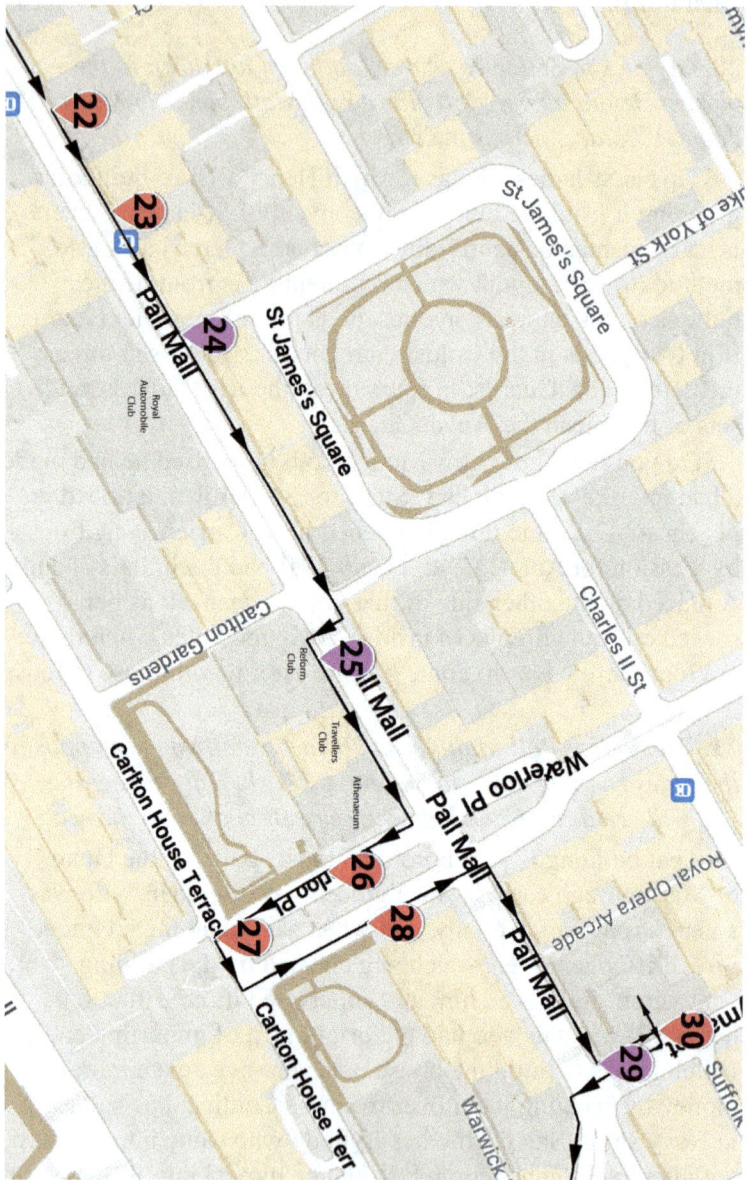

In the nineteenth century, Marlborough House became a secondary royal residence, occupied by the Prince of Wales, then by his widow, Queen Alexandra, followed by Queen Mary later. Hence the next story.

**22.** *Continue along the left-hand side of Pall Mall for about forty yards till you come to a large and impressive building, across the street on your right, with four pillars beside the doorway. At the top of the pillars are two sets of badges. The two blue badges have an open book on them, the two red badges show a closed book with a lion in each quarter.*

This is the Oxford and Cambridge Club. Look at the pillars by the doorway: the blue shields above them are Oxford, the red shields are Cambridge. Our version is that the Oxford badge shows the book of knowledge with the three crowns of theology, law, and medicine, while the Cambridge badge has four lions keeping the book of knowledge firmly shut. Their version is that the four Cambridge lions are keeping the book of knowledge safe while Oxford are still struggling with the first page.

With one exception, every building along the south side of Pall Mall belongs to the Crown Estate and is administered by the Estate Commissioners. Many years ago I heard a story which is probably apocryphal, but I'll tell it anyway. When they granted a building lease to the club here in 1836, the Commissioners laid down the condition that the windows at the back overlooking Marlborough House should be of frosted glass. Well, you didn't want licentious club men looking into the private apartments of royalty, did you? The club had to accept the conditions, and they lived with it for many years.

In the 1920s, so the story went, the members became fed up with their frosted glass and approached the Commissioners, who turned them down flat. But then someone had the bright idea of inviting the Prince of Wales (later Duke of Windsor) to become a member. He was duly elected, came to the club, expressed surprise at the frosted glass, and was promptly asked if he would approach the Commissioners to get the ruling lifted. He did so, but that didn't work either.

Then he had a bright idea: the club should invite Queen Mary to lunch and see what she thought about it. It worked out perfectly. She came, she toured the club from top to bottom, expressed horror at the frosted glass – and, Queen Mary being who she was, the Commissioners changed their minds.

The official version is that the club simply wanted to build an extension in 1928, a proposal rejected outright by the Commissioners. The club went over their heads by inviting the Royal Family to lunch and secured their approval to the scheme, and the Commissioners had to change their minds. Same story, I suppose, but mine is more fun.

Along the balustrade that separates the club house from the street are a series of thin black iron pillars with a small dished circle on top of them; there are several more further along Pall Mall. If you read Victorian novels, you often see some such phrase as: "England rejoiced and that night the flambeaux flared along Pall Mall." Those are flambeaux – gas flares lit on special occasions, nowadays usually when a club has its big annual dinner. I have seen them lit, and it is quite an experience. A three- or four-foot flame shoots out from each, making a splendid display, and it is appropriate they are here since, in 1807, this was the first street in England to be lit by gas.

**23.** *Continue along the left-hand side of Pall Mall till you see No. 79 on the other side of the road. It bears a blue plaque.*

The blue plaque marks the site of the home of Nell Gwynne, Charles II's mistress. I mentioned just now that the Crown Estates own the south side of Pall Mall, with one exception. This is it, the only freehold along that side of the street. Nell Gwynne, originally an orange seller at the Drury Lane theatre, became Charles II's mistress in 1668, had two sons by him, and, as any girl would, wanted security for her old age. Charles gave her a lifetime lease on a house here, but that wasn't good enough. She allegedly made her views clear with the words: "I have conveyed freely under the Crown these many years. Surely the Crown can convey freely to me." Whatever words she used, they worked, and she was able to leave the house to her son as she hoped. The present building replaced it around 1850.

Just past Nell Gwynne's house is a splendid red-brick house with a pillared portico over its doorway. This is Schomberg House, the last of the seventeenth-century houses that once lined the street. It is named after Marshal Schomberg, who came over as second-in-command to William of Orange in 1688. It is an impressive building, though one half of it was demolished back in the 1860s. There is a puzzle for you here. About 1970, an architect named C.H. Elsom was given some architectural award, and during the speeches afterwards, he was asked to name the building of which he was most proud. Elsom was renowned for working in the modern style – glass, steel, and tower blocks – and there was astonishment among the audience when he answered. He said the project of which he was most proud was that, in 1956, he had re-built the long-demolished wing of Schomberg House so successfully that people could not tell which wing was his.

Can you see which side he built? Look at both wings closely. Then look at the Parking sign to the right of the doorway. Got it? Then look at the window on the first floor directly

above the sign. Look at the brickwork supporting the window. See how it drops half an inch or so to the right? The right-hand side is the original, the left-hand side was completely replaced by Elsom in 1956, and I reckon he made a marvellous job of it.


**24.** *Continue on along Pall Mall to the corner where the road runs up to St James's Square on your left. Stop here.*

I'm sure you remember Rupert Baxter, the suspicious killjoy secretary at Blandings Castle. I wondered for a long time where his name came from, and I believe it is from an association of ideas. You know the way certain parts of the country have their local heroes – John Bunyan in Bedford Jail, Robin Hood in Nottingham, that sort of thing. If Rupert Baxter, that Puritan killjoy, got his name from anywhere, I reckon it was Wodehouse's memory of Richard Baxter. Baxter, a famous Puritan hellfire preacher of the late seventeenth century, is the local historic figure associated with Bridgnorth in Shropshire, where Wodehouse lived as a boy. Baxter's house is still there and is open to the public. I mention him now because, in 1680, he came here to St James's Square, then the smartest address in London, and delivered a stirring sermon from the middle of the square. He did so because, as he said: "Like the Americans, they have not heard a proper sermon these ten years."

Across Pall Mall from you now is the Royal Automobile Club, the RAC. It is, I believe, London's largest club, and at one stage it had its own post office, miniature rifle range, and Turkish baths, as well as a swimming pool and squash courts. I had lunch there once, and I was puzzled by the decor of the dining room. I couldn't put my finger on it, but it worried me so much that I did some homework.

The RAC was simply the Automobile Club of Great Britain until 1907, when Edward VII gave them the right to call themselves Royal. It is said that he had been very impressed by his visit to the Automobile Club de France and, so the story goes, he told the Automobile Club committee that they could call themselves Royal if they built an impressive clubhouse as the French had done in Paris. The story also goes on to say that the King made it clear he wanted the London club to be just like the Paris club.

Whatever the reason, the RAC promptly employed Messrs Mewes and Davis, who had just completed the Paris and London Ritz hotels. Davis, an English architect trained in Paris, was responsible for the main construction side while Mewes, a Frenchman, did the décor. That is why I was so puzzled by the dining room. I was used to the English version of the French Second Empire architectural style (very popular in England from 1860 onwards), but there was a marked difference when it was designed by a French architect. As far as I can ascertain, all the decoration, plasterwork, etc., were carried out by French workmen, including what one might call the crowning indignity.

Look up at the triangular pediment at the top of the building. See the woman in the middle who represents the Spirit of Speed or something like it? Now look closely at the small figure to the right, as you look at her. It is a cherub riding a motor car, and it is not even a British car on top of Britain's senior car club. It is a 1909 French Renault!

**25.** *Stay on the left-hand side of Pall Mall till you come to the next street junction on your left. Cross over to the other side of the street, then turn left to continue your way along Pall Mall. The three large buildings on your right are three famous clubhouses.*

The first clubhouse you come to (*on the corner of Pall Mall and Carlton Gardens*) is the Reform Club, built in 1832 by Charles Barry as a copy of the Farnese Palace in Rome. The kitchens of the Reform Club were designed by the famous chef Charles Soyer, who installed the first gas stoves seen in the country, and his menus were the talk of London. In 1847 the Reform Act lent him to the Government to assist in feeding the Irish during the Great Famine, and in 1855 he was sent to the Crimea to advise the British army on cooking in the field. It was there that he invented the Soyer stove, a field kitchen that remained in use till the Falklands Islands campaign nearly 130 years later.

The next building along is the Travellers' Club, also built by Barry in 1832, copying the Palazzo Pandolfini in Florence (a surprising number of London buildings are copies of Continental originals, including Buckingham Palace). Two things to note here, both at the bottom of the steps. The first is the boot-scraper on the right. Common enough once, it is a reminder of the days when horses were the main form of transport. In the 1880s, for example, 20,000 horses crossed London Bridge every 24 hours, and every horse produced

40 pounds of 'droppings' a day. That is why London streets were so filthy, why street crossing-sweepers were so busy, and gentlemen had turn-ups on their trousers – and why we needed boot-scrapers like these.

At the left-hand side of the steps is a much more mysterious object: a small, spiked railing protecting the angle in the stonework. You will see versions of this all the way down Whitehall. As far as I know, my book of London walks was the first to identify this odd feature; I'm very proud of that. To put it bluntly, railings were commonly placed in angles like this because there were no public lavatories in London until the 1850s. Think about it. If someone feels a sudden urge and has to go, then corners like these were the natural place to, shall we say, relieve the pressure. So these spiked railings were put here to make access to corners more difficult. I call them 'Commit No Nuisance rails' because I can think of no better term.

The next building, which takes us up to Waterloo Place, is the Athenaeum Club. Wodehouse referred to it occasionally but usually gave it another name such as the Demosthenes, Antiquarian, or Mausoleum Club; he had also had no hesitation in placing it opposite the Drones if the plot required it (*Cocktail Time*). It is clearly Lord Uffenham's club in *Money in the Bank* when he descends the broad staircase "with one hand glued to the arm of a worried-looking bishop with whom he was discussing Supralapsarianism". While White's has long been famous as London's smartest club, the Athenaeum is famous for its intellectual membership. When you become head of an Oxford college, a Permanent Under Secretary, or a bishop, someone will suggest you join the Athenaeum. I remember how impressed I was when I read that it had four libraries, of which one was for the staff. I was even more impressed when I saw the plaque they put over the cellar access in the 1930s.

**26.** *Turn right, pass the entrance to the Athenaeum, and immediately past that are steps down to the cellar.*

If the Virginia creeper has been cut back, you can see the concrete plaque on the wall above the doorway has three lines of Greek which, I am sure, you will immediately recognise as coming from Homer's *Odyssey*. They are the words with which Nausicaa addressed Odysseus when she found him washed up on the shore: "Come to my father's house so I may offer you refreshment." Don't mock it. When it was placed here, I would bet that half the members could translate it on sight.

On the edge of the pavement is a mounting block erected specifically for the Duke of Wellington. When the Athenaeum was founded, the Duke was persuaded to join but also made a point of joining the United Service Club across the road. Rather than show favouritism, he insisted on a similar mounting block being placed over there as well. If you wonder what the point of the mounting block was, the Duke disliked riding in carriages and rode round London on horseback as long as he was physically able to do so.

**27.** *Keep on the right-hand side of Waterloo Place and make your way down to the end, heading for a single tree in a small patch of greenery between the steps down to the park and the large building on the right.*

The large building on your right is now the home of the Royal Society but was the German embassy till 1939. It has an unusual interior: it is the only building outside Germany remodelled by the architect Albert Speer, Hitler's efficient minister of works. I have been inside, and it is quite extraordinary – exactly as one remembers pictures of Nazi offices: enormous rooms and doorways above which one can still imagine the swastikas that used to adorn them.

At the base of the tree in the little green patch beside the Royal Society is another, very different, German relic. A small wooden frame with a glass front protects a dog's grave. During the Blitz in the last war, the American broadcaster Edward R. Murrow said he learned what the English people were really like when he found this grave to Giro, the dog belonging to von Hoesch, the German ambassador before Ribbentrop. The dog died in 1934, and Murrow said how impressed he was that, though the Germans were killing Londoners every night, no one ever thought of damaging the gravestone to a German dog. In fact, the reverse applied: they protected it from damage.

And the nice thing is – we still do. This little spot is where they stack all the scaffolding and flagpoles when they have processions down the Mall, but when they do, the first thing to arrive is a strong iron box which is placed over the dog's grave here before anything else is allowed in!

Immediately to your left are railings and gates guarding the steps down to the Mall. Why are they there? Around 1853, William Gladstone, then Chancellor of the Exchequer, was standing on the steps of the Athenaeum behind us chatting to somebody when they heard shouts and screams up the road towards Piccadilly. A horse had bolted and was galloping down the slope, while in the carriage behind it a frantic mother held on to her terrified child. Gladstone, then a strong, vigorous man, dashed across the road, seized the horse's reins and dragged it to a halt just before it reached these steps down to the Mall. That afternoon, he returned to the House of Commons and had a quiet word with the Crown Estates Commissioners. The railings were erected a week later.

The enormous column above you commemorates the Duke of York, second son of George III. He is the original of the nursery rhyme: "The Grand Old Duke of York, he had ten thousand men." As with many nursery rhymes, it is based on fact. In 1793 the Duke commanded a British army fighting the French in the Netherlands. He was not a good tactician and won no battles, but he did what no one had done before: he kept his army healthy. He was a superb administrator and founded schools and orphanages for soldiers' children. He realised that the Netherlands' low-lying swamps and marshes would soon reduce the numbers of his army far more effectively than the French would, so he moved camp frequently to ensure no diseases could take hold. As you can imagine, this made him highly unpopular with his soldiers. What they wanted was to get settled in, get to know the local pubs, and, more important, get to know the local girls. But just as they were beginning to do so, off they moved again. The nursery rhyme grew out of resentment at his apparently pointless manoeuvres around the Netherlands, but historians now believe he saved the lives of thousands by doing so.

**28.** *Turn left and make your way back up the other side of Waterloo Place. Stop halfway along by the statue of Captain Scott on your right.*

This statue of Captain Scott, who died in the Antarctic in 1912, is worth noting as the only statue in London done by the subject's widow. Scott's wife, a sculptress, saw it unveiled here in 1915. A few feet away from you is the mounting block installed for the Duke of Wellington, matching the block outside the Athenaeum across the road, and this is the best place to admire the trick worked by John Wilson Croker on the Athenaeum Club in 1827.

If you look at the Athenaeum from here, you can see the frieze running round the building just below the roof. It is a representation of the Elgin marbles, which had recently been brought to England, and it is there through the determination and cunning of John Wilson Croker (1780–1857). Croker was one of those brilliant, if unscrupulous, individuals you prefer to read about rather than work with. A politician, he was made secretary to the Navy Board, a post in which he performed very efficiently for twenty years. He was a leading figure in the creation of the Athenaeum Club and decided that, with its classical name, the club needed a frieze copying the carvings from the Parthenon. He persuaded the committee to open a subscription list for this, but the response was disappointing, to say the least. Not a bit discouraged, Croker immediately posted another notice, seeking funds for an icehouse in the garden of the club to keep meat fresh. The members thought this was a splendid idea, and the subscriptions poured in, which Croker promptly used for his original purpose.

The contemporary comment was:

> I'm John Wilson Croker,
> I do as I please.
> They wanted an ice-house;
> I gave them a frieze.

The building immediately on your right was, until 1976, the United Service Club. It was built at the same time as the Athenaeum, and the rivalry between the two was strong.

The Athenaeum members allegedly disliked the bloodthirsty generals and admirals of the United Service, while the gallant soldiers and sailors here had no time for the hypocritical bishops and know-all intellectuals of the Athenaeum. This building is now the Institute of Directors since the United Service had to close in 1976, but they left behind at least one good story.

The Kaiser, grandson of Queen Victoria, was made an honorary field-marshal in 1904, which meant he automatically became a member of the United Service Club. His portrait was put up in the dining room – but then the First World War came along. What do you do with a painting of a foreign monarch with whom you are at war but who, under the club rules, is still a member of your club? You put it in the servants' quarters until the war is over, of course. What else?

**29.** *Continue up to the zebra crossing ahead of you, cross over to the other side of Pall Mall, and turn right. Make your way along to the Haymarket and pause on the corner, under the canopy of New Zealand House.*

New Zealand House stands on the site of the Carlton Hotel, which was bombed during the war. Wodehouse mentioned the Carlton in eleven stories; with the Berkeley, it was the smart place to have lunch in the 1920s and 1930s. But we are popping in to look at something else: London's only home-grown totem pole. Officially it is called a pouhi (pronounced 'poo-ee'), not a totem pole, but you'll see why I use the term.

Inia Te Wiata (1915–71) was a Maori singer who was also a trained woodcarver. He had begun singing in church choirs in New Zealand, and in 1947 he was awarded a scholarship to come to London and be trained professionally. He sang at Covent Garden and made quite a reputation for himself. When New Zealand House was being built, he realised he could make some return for the help and encouragement he had received. In the cellars of this building, he began to carve an enormous pouhi. He could only work on it between singing engagements, and he died in 1971 before it was completed, but his sons finished off the last section.

It is not a Wodehouse story, but when you see the pouhi, I think you will be as impressed as I was by its sheer size and the incongruity of a Covent Garden singer spending his free time over eight years working away in the cellar here to carve it.

**30.** *Turn left up the Haymarket and enter the door into the lobby of New Zealand House. The pouhi is some ten yards over to the right, rearing up towards the roof. An explanatory plaque is on the wall in the far right-hand corner.*

After you have admired the pouhi, come out of New Zealand House and take a look at the Theatre Royal, Haymarket, up the road to your left. You will see the name 'Theatre Royal' on theatres up and down the country. As far as I can ascertain, the term stems from the days when companies of actors needed a licence to perform and theatres were very closely controlled by the authorities. In the 1760s, an actor named Samuel Foote acquired the tenancy of the Theatre Royal Haymarket, but he was unable to get the licence to stage plays. His satires of his fellow actors had made him many enemies, and his attacks on politicians had not made him popular with the authorities, either. He tried various tricks to get past the law, charging audiences for a cup of coffee and showing them the play for free, that sort of thing, but it didn't work, and he became desperate to get the necessary licence, which had to come from the Duke of York.

I cannot guarantee the veracity of the story, but it was widely alleged that Foote harassed the Duke for so long that, at last, the Duke promised to give him his licence if he rode a certain horse for ten minutes. Foote couldn't ride, and the horse was unbroken, but he was desperate. He mounted the steed, was promptly thrown off, and broke his leg. Horrified at the incident, the Duke's companions reproached him so much that Foote was granted his licence as compensation.

And that, so the story goes, is why actors wish each other good luck with the expression "Break a leg".

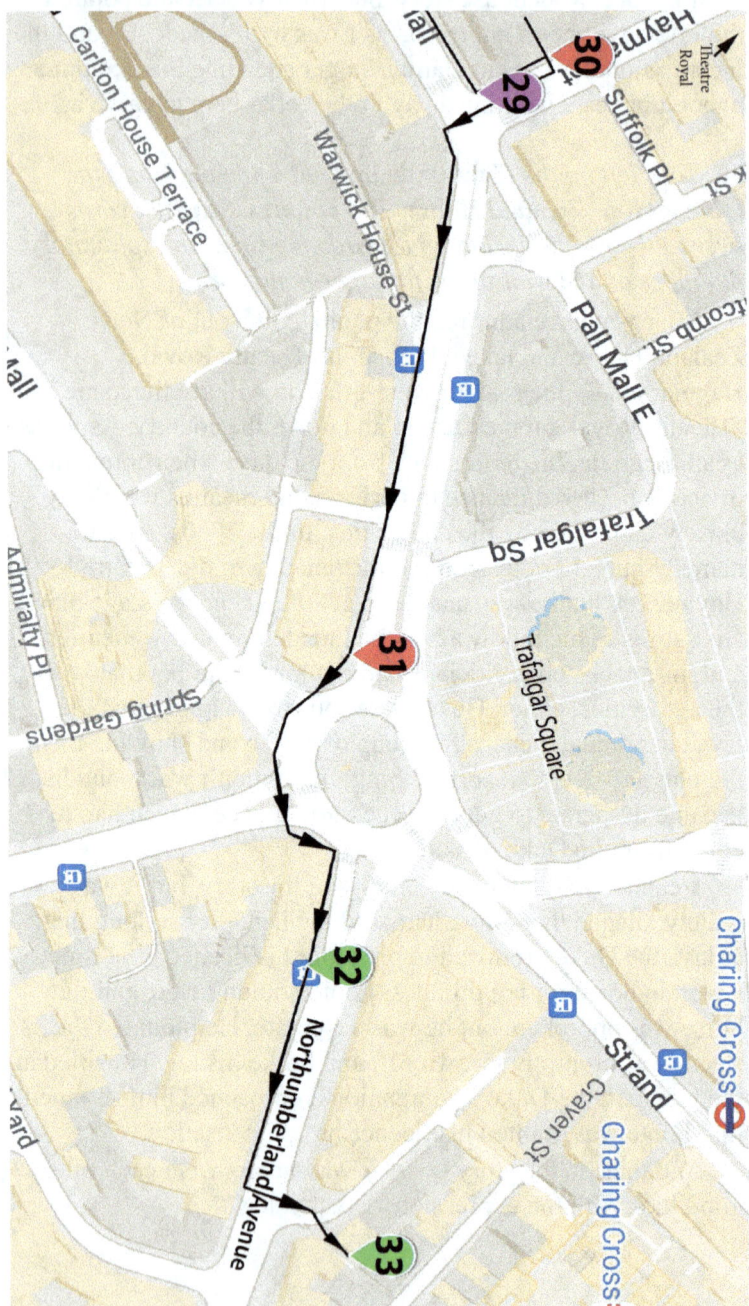

**31.** *Turn right, make your way over the crossing, turn left, and walk along Cockspur Street to Trafalgar. The doorway of Uganda House, on the corner by The Mall, is an excellent spot to consider the history of Trafalgar Square.*

### a. The Centre of London

If you ask people where the official centre of London is, you will get a variety of answers. The Mansion House, St Paul's, or Piccadilly Circus are favourite guesses, but the centre of London is just over to your right, a small brass plate set in the ground about twenty feet north of the statue of Charles I on his horse.

The reason the plate is here goes back nearly a thousand years. In 1042, when Edward the Confessor became king, his court was secure from attack behind the walls of the city of London which the Romans had built

*(Photo courtesy of Robert Bruce)*

and which Alfred the Great had later renewed. Edward was a very devout man, and it is believed he had made a vow that, if he became king, he would make a pilgrimage to St Peter's in Rome. It was clear, however, that if he did so, he would not come back as king; there were far too many rival claimants around. Legend goes on to say that he became more and more worried about breaking his oath until his councillors showed him a way out. If he were to build a great church to St Peter, this would absolve him from guilt – and there happened to be a small chapel dedicated to St Peter just two miles away, ripe for rebuilding

Edward seized on the idea and promptly began to build the new church down at Thorney Island, where an offshoot of the Tyburn runs into the Thames. To make sure the job was done properly, he moved his court out of the City and built himself a new palace beside the abbey he was building. He got the job done just in time. Eight days after the abbey church of St Peter was consecrated, it saw Edward's funeral. Before the end of the year, William the Conqueror was crowned king in what was by then known as the West Minster abbey, and he moved into Edward's palace of Westminster.

The merchants in the City decided to stay exactly where they were, behind their nice, safe walls. They saw no reason to move just because the king had a religious obsession. And that is how things remained for a couple of hundred years, with the merchants in the City and the king down in his Westminster Palace. In the middle of the thirteenth century, a body called the Parliament came into existence and met at the Palace of Westminster, but it remained a Royal residence till the sixteenth century, when Henry VIII took over Cardinal Wolsey's Whitehall Palace up the road and moved in there, taking his officials with him but leaving the Parliament behind. Whitehall remained the main Royal palace till it burned down in 1698, when the king moved to St James's Palace, but this time he left his officials, the civil servants, behind in Whitehall.

Now you know why the business centre is in the City, why Parliament occupies the Palace of Westminster, and why the civil servants are in Whitehall. Through all that time, if you wanted to get from the City to Westminster, you either came by river or made your way along Fleet Street and the Strand to the corner here at Charing Cross. Not until they built the Embankment in 1870 was it possible to go any other way. And that is why that small plaque is the centre of London.

In addition to being a historic landmark, it also has a financial significance. Because of the extra expense of working in central London, Government employees are given a small allowance if they work within a six-mile radius of this plaque. When I was working in the Ministry of Defence in Whitehall, it was about 40 pence a day – not much but better than nothing.

## b. Trafalgar Square

You will find surprisingly little mention of Trafalgar Square in books on architecture, and I believe the reason is because the architects involved were told firmly what to do. By 1800, this area had become a squalid locality full of small alleys, hovels, and shanties, and it was such a disgrace that everybody welcomed John Nash's suggestion in 1819 to clear the site to create better access between the Strand and Regent Street. When they had done so, all that was left was an old army stables on the site of the National Gallery and the church of St Martin-in-the-Fields up in the top right corner.

The first building on the new Square was Canada House over on the left, built in 1822 by Smirke, with the Union Club occupying the nearer left-hand side and the Royal College of Physicians at the other end. It was built to a basic design approved by the Crown Estates Commissioners, who then owned the site.

When, later in the 1820s, a competition was held to design the National Gallery, the winner, William Wilkins, was called in by the Crown Commissioners and directed to make certain 'minor adjustments' to his design. Firstly, the roofline was to resemble that of the old Army stables it was replacing. That is why there are those 'pepper pots' on top, replacing the foul air vents from the old stables. Secondly, he was to lower the roofline to match that of St Martin's Church. Thirdly, he was to move the Gallery back so there was a clear access to the front of St Martin's. Fourthly, he was to reduce the depth of the building to allow for a new barracks to be built behind it. Fifthly, the frontage was to be not brick but Portland Stone, to match St Martin's. Sixthly, he was to put pillars along the front, firstly to match St Martin's and, secondly, because George IV had had them lying around since he had demolished Carlton House and wanted to find a use for them. And finally, the roofline was to have a balustrade that matched St Martin's as well. Apart from that, he could do whatever he liked! So he built the National Gallery we see today.

Another hundred years went by, and Sir Herbert Baker, who had built the South African Parliament building and much of New Delhi, was asked to build South Africa House over there on the right. He had firm views on the matter, but so did the Commissioners. Hence the Portland stone frontage of South Africa House to match St Martin's, the matching pillars, and the matching rooftop balustrade.

See the pattern right round the Square? That is why Londoners love it and so many architects hate it: they were told firmly what to do.

### c. Nelson's Column

From the moment the Square was proposed, there was argument over what to put in it. One proposal was to build a copy of the Great Pyramid as a memorial to those who died in the Napoleonic Wars. Another suggestion was that a copy of the Colosseum in Rome should be built here, and all the scientific and learned societies should be compulsorily moved into it. The enforced propinquity, it was believed, would lead to better understanding among doctors, scientists, architects, etc., and lead to a new Golden Age of education and scientific progress. Not until 1837, four years after the Square had been laid out, did someone suggest a memorial to Nelson. Everybody thought this was a splendid idea, and designs poured in from all over the country.

One man suggested building a copy of the Parthenon with a statue of Nelson on top; another wanted a Gothic cathedral built here with Nelson on top of the spire; while somebody else wanted an enormous model of the globe, tilted over so that England was on top with a statue of Nelson on top of that. One idea I like was to build a copy of Nelson's flagship in stone, twice life-size, with every sailor on it modelled in bronze, doing whatever they were doing when Nelson was shot. It took a year for the committee to make their decision. They took the safe way out – when in doubt, go classical – and accepted William Railton's design based on the pillars in the temple of Mars Ultor in Rome. They stipulated one condition: that the column was to be at least 30 feet higher than the recently erected column for the Duke of York. Another decision, which I think they regretted later, was to split the job up amongst several artists and sculptors.

Mr Railton got the job of building the column itself but made slow progress on it, and it was not completed till 1842. Then a Mr Smith took over the next task, designing and affixing the pieces of the bronze capital made from guns used

52

in the Napoleonic Wars. That took another year, but Mr Smith celebrated its completion by giving a dinner party for fourteen friends on top! The next step was the installation of the Nelson statue. It was brought through the streets in two sections and, watched by cheering crowds, the sections were slowly pulled to the top. Unfortunately, they did not fit properly and the cheers turned to boos as they were ignominiously brought down again. They were put in place a couple of months later with a minimum of publicity.

Londoners then had to wait another six years, until 1849, for the four enormous bronze panels around the base which depict the battles of Copenhagen, the Nile, Cape St Vincent, and Trafalgar. Each is by a different artist, they are of different sizes, and there was some excuse for the delay. When they were commissioned, there was no foundry in Europe capable of making castings this size. But they arrived at last, and all Londoners had to wait for now were the bronze lions at the base. It turned out to be a long wait.

Cartoonists and comedians had a field day making jokes about the delay, but the authorities could do little about it. They had rejected the first lions submitted as being far too small and had approached Sir Edwin Landseer, the most popular artist of the day. Although his Stag at Bay and other paintings were known across the country, Landseer was most unwilling to do it, pointing out that he was a painter, not a sculptor, but pressure was brought to bear. Eventually, when Queen Victoria herself told him she was "most anxious" he undertake the job, he agreed to do so – on one condition. He insisted he needed a real lion to work from, and the authorities had to agree. It was some years before a lion died in the Zoo and was promptly put on a cart, taken across London, and dumped in Landseer's studio in St John's Wood. No one knows how long it was there, but it was long enough for the servants to give notice, his wife and family to move out, and the neighbours to complain to the sanitary authorities. But at last, in 1867, only 30 years late, the lions were installed.

And the Square is still unfinished today. There are statues all round the Square, but the plinth up in the top left-hand corner remained vacant for 160 years until 1999. In that year, we saw the first of the very 'modern' sculptures which are placed here for periods of eighteen to twenty-four months or so. They are meant to represent modern art in its various forms, a laudable aim, but there is a strong body of opinion that thinks they are here only because, even after 170 years, nobody can agree on a permanent occupant of the site!

And there's another piece of unfinished business. Down at the end of the balustrade that runs down the left-hand side of the Square is an unusual lamp on top of a little turret. Its twin is over on the right-hand corner. The lamp has twelve faces to it, and the theory is that its shape means that light is emitted more efficiently. They are known as Panopticon lamps and there were placed here as an experiment in the 1860s. A decision on the experiment is still awaited.

### d. Two more stories and we'll move on.

Look at St Martin-in-the-Field, the hub around which the Square was designed. If you are American, it should seem very familiar. James Gibbs built it in 1722–24, and it was a sensation. Gibbs got the idea from the Roman temple at Nîmes in France, but then put a steeple on top of it at the wrong end. In this country the steeple was always placed over the altar, not over the west door, but the style took off and has been copied all over the world. Three of Gibbs's assistants realised something else as well. This design can be built as easily in timber as in brick or stone, and they went over to America and introduced the style in New England. The New Englanders liked it, and as they moved west across the country, they took the style with them; you can see copies of it all over the US. That is why, when the hero in a Western walks down the street to fight the baddie, the church you often see behind him is a copy of St Martin's. If you are wondering why there is a royal coat of arms over the entrance, it is because this is the parish church for Buckingham Palace, and all the royal births are registered here. And if you wonder why the clock has a blue face and gold figures, the reason is that back in the 16th century Henry VIII said that was the way he wanted church clocks to look.

54

The statue of Charles I on his horse, over to your right, the first equestrian statue in England, was done by Hubert Le Sueur in 1633 for the Earl of Bedford. It stood in Covent Garden till the end of the Civil War, when the victorious Parliamentarians sold it for scrap to a brass worker with the incredibly appropriate name of Mr Rivett. Mr Rivett purportedly melted the statue down and made a lot of money selling knives and knick-knacks to Parliamentarians as mementos of their victory and to Royalists as mementos of their dead king. When Charles II was restored to the throne in 1660, Mr Rivett brought off another financial coup by producing the statue and selling it to the king. It was installed here at Charing Cross after some formalities that included the execution of some of the men who had killed Charles I. Pepys made an unforgettable entry in his diary for 13 October 1660: "I went out to Charing Cross, to see Major-general Harrison hanged, drawn and quartered; which was done there, he looking as cheerful as any man could do in that condition."

That's enough about Trafalgar Square. Let's get back to Wodehouse.

**32.** *Cross Whitehall, bear left, and then turn immediately right to enter Northumberland Avenue. Stop outside the café about twenty yards down on the right-hand side.*

We are now in Northumberland Avenue, looking across the road at the large office building they put up in 1964 to replace the Constitutional Club. Wodehouse drew it as the 'Senior Conservative Club', whose members included Lord Emsworth and Rupert Psmith. Wodehouse was a member of the Constitutional from about 1905 or so, and it was exactly as he described, a large, impersonal, respectable club, noted for its enormous marble staircase and its excellent cuisine. Wodehouse mentioned his membership in the preface to *The Girl on the Boat*, and in 'A Tithe for Charity' he confirmed that the Senior Conservative Club stood here.

A condition of building this new block was that the façade of the Constitutional had to be copied. That is why, up there on the first floor, you can see a single bow window, copying the bow window of the old club dining room. Now, cast your mind back to Lord Emsworth meeting Psmith in *Leave It to* Psmith. Lord Emsworth, having recovered his spectacles, was entranced by the sight of a florist this side of the road and dashed over to consult with the shop owner. It should come as no surprise that there was a florist here in the 1920s and '30s.

Over the years, I noticed how often Wodehouse wrote about his difficulty in finding plots for his stories, and how many he got from his friend Bill Townend. I also noticed that many incidents in his life later appeared in his stories – minor events in themselves, but enough to give him an idea to expand and develop. If you've read *Psmith in the City*, you will recall that it involves a battle of wills between Psmith, a new bank clerk, and the bank's general manager. Psmith happened to be a member of the same club as the manager, and that enabled him to come out victorious. Unusual but not impossible, so I did some homework. I discovered that the chairman of the Hong Kong and Shanghai Bank when Wodehouse as a clerk there was Sir Ewan Cameron. I also discovered that, firstly, he had political ambitions; secondly and more importantly, he was a member of only one club. You've guessed it – the Constitutional, the same club as his very junior clerk, P.G. Wodehouse.

And now for our last Wodehouse site.

**33.** *Cross Northumberland Avenue and walk down the left-hand side to the corner. Turn left and walk up the alley beside the Sherlock Holmes pub. Opposite the pub side door, stop and look at the building immediately to your right.*

If you have read Psmith in the City, you will remember that Psmith blackmails Mr Bickersdyke in the Turkish Baths, which were a few yards from their club (the Constitutional / 'Senior

Conservative'). This ornate doorway is all that remains of the Turkish Baths that Psmith, Mr Bickersdyke, and Wodehouse himself used all those years ago.

When I found it, about a month before the first Wodehouse Pilgrimage in 1989, I charged into the building, then a branch of Barclay's Bank, asking to see the manager. I started telling him all about it, when he interrupted me: "A Turkish Bath! That's what it was! Thank Heaven you came in." He explained that they had just done some work on the offices at the back, had taken down a false ceiling and found above it a dome painted blue and decorated with stars, and they were wondering on earth it was when I arrived to tell them. The result was that when I brought the Wodehouse Pilgrims the following month, we were treated like royalty with coffee and biscuits all round.

**34.** *The walk finishes here outside the Sherlock Holmes pub, which deserves a mention as well, since Wodehouse had a great admiration for Arthur Conan Doyle. Doyle was also a member of the Constitutional Club, and he and Wodehouse used to lunch there together. Doyle also used the Baths in his stories: see the opening of 'The Illustrious Client'.*

In 1951 we had the Festival of Britain, a series of exhibitions, fairs, and other events to cheer ourselves up after the war. It was my last year at school, and I went along to the main site on the South Bank, with the just-completed Festival Hall as its centre. One exhibit was a re-creation of Sherlock Holmes's room in 221B Baker Street. When the Festival was over, the exhibit was going to be dismantled, but somebody in Whitbread's brewery knew his Conan Doyle and persuaded the brewery to buy it. He had remembered that, in *The Hound of the Baskervilles*, Holmes traced Sir Henry Baskerville's movements and, from a receipt in his pocket, found that he had stayed at the Northumberland Hotel at Charing Cross.

This was the real Northumberland Hotel, as Conan Doyle knew very well, so Whitbread's installed the Sherlock Holmes sitting-room here, changed the name of the pub, and filled it with Holmesean memorabilia. If you go through the side door here, straight up the stairs, turn left, and go along to the end, you will find Holmes's sitting room exactly as Doyle described. After which, I suggest you return downstairs to the bar and reward yourself with a drink after your walk.

*The Author and Wodehouse fan Doug Jeffords*
*preparing to enter the pub after a satisfying walk.*

# Walk 2

# The London of Gally Threepwood
# and Stanley Ukridge

## *Introduction*

The first Wodehouse Walk through Mayfair to Northumberland Avenue is based on the London Wodehouse knew in the 1920s: Bertie Wooster's West End, the Drones, and the famous venerable clubs of St James's Street and Pall Mall. On this walk we look at an earlier London – Gally Threepwood's and Stanley Ukridge's London – which Wodehouse knew between 1900 and 1914. After two years in the Hong Kong and Shanghai Bank, he became a freelance writer in 1902, then joined the *Globe* evening newspaper and saw his stories published in *The Captain*, *Pearson's Magazine*, and the famous *Strand*. This was when he met members of the by-then-defunct Pelican Club, started writing lyrics for musical comedies, was employed at the legendary Gaiety Theatre, and went around London with Herbert Westbrook (the main source of Stanley Ukridge), Bill Townend, and other impecunious young men. The walk finishes at a London pub Wodehouse knew, one of the four he mentioned in his stories that are still in existence.

## *The Walk*   *(Maps on pages 60, 66, 74)*

**1.** *If you are walking with somebody, I suggest meeting downstairs in Piccadilly Circus Underground Station by the World Time Clock Map. Take the exit marked 'Subway 4' and walk up the first flight of steps on the right, marked 'Shaftesbury Avenue'. Stop just beyond the top of the steps.*

Across the road is the Criterion, built in the 1870s as an enormous restaurant/theatre complex. The theatre is underground and remarkable for its decoration, still unchanged from those days. The restaurant a few yards to the left of the theatre was once the famous Criterion Bar, which Gally Threepwood frequented and where Beach's niece, Maudie

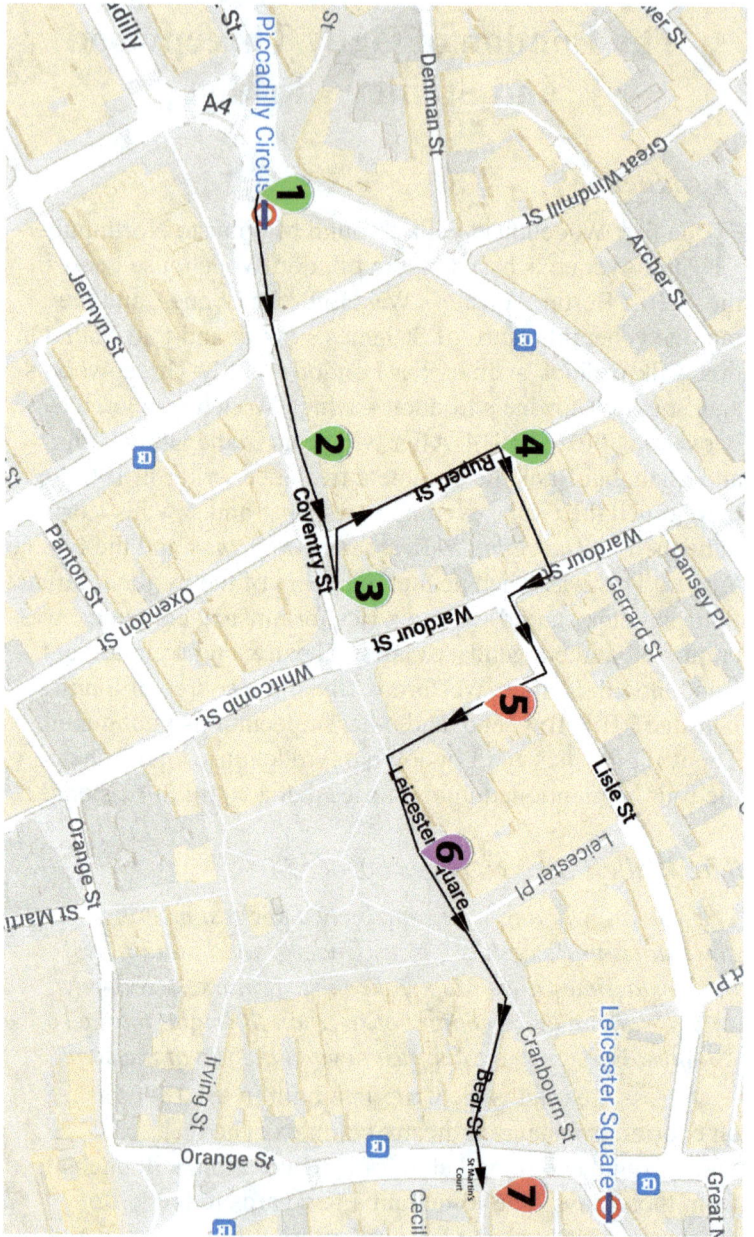

Montrose – later Lady Parsloe – worked behind the beer-pumps. It had a mixed reputation as a popular spot for young men visiting London and was equally popular with the con men and tricksters who preyed on them.

Until a few years ago, there was still an enormous American eagle on the wall. I understand it was there because this was London's first so-called American bar, i.e. a long bar running the length of one enormous room as opposed to the separate public bar, saloon bar and private bar that you got in most English pubs then. It has now become an expensive restaurant, but, happily, there is still a long bar.

The enormous building looming up immediately beside you is the London Pavilion, now joined to the Trocadero a few yards further on. The Trocadero, which opened in 1896 as London's first popular large restaurant, features as the Bandolero Restaurant in *Uneasy Money*; Lord Dawlish lunched with Claire Fenwick here in the opening chapter.

*(The Trocadero closed in 1965 and subsequently became a venue for entertainment and exhibitions. It now houses the Crystal Maze LIVE Experience.)*

**2.** *Walk along Coventry Street towards Leicester Square, with the Trocadero building on your left. As you pass Shaver's Place, a narrow lane across the street on your right (easy to miss), a restaurant is on your immediate left. (Note: In the 2009 edition of this book, there was a music shop here. As of 2023, the location is the Haidilao Hot Pot.)*

The doorway of the restaurant beside you covers what was once the narrow entrance to Arundell Street, the setting for the opening chapter of *Something Fresh*. Located directly across from Shaver's Place, it was a short cul-de-sac that widened out into a small square with two hotels facing each other, the Hotels Mathis and Previtali, exactly as PGW told us. The grandson of the owners told us about them in *Wooster Sauce* (No. 16, Dec. 2000, p.8; and No. 17, Mar. 2001, p.8). At the end of the square were three small houses, owned by people who advertised 'apartments', i.e. lodgings, for young men and women who wanted cheap accommodation in London.

The middle house, No. 7, owned by Mrs Austin, was where Bill Townend took rooms in late 1905 or early 1906 with the £10 Wodehouse had given him from the £31 advance he got for *Love Among the Chickens*. Wodehouse did so because Townend had told him the original story about a man called Craxton who had tried chicken-farming with the same disastrous results. In *Something Fresh*, Wodehouse put Ashe Marson in Townend's rooms.

Sometime after Bill Townend moved in, another friend of Wodehouse's, Herbert Westbrook, the man who became the main source of Ukridge, moved into the rooms above Townend. That is why Ukridge was given rooms here in the short stories 'Return of Battling Billson' and 'A Bit of Luck for Mabel' – two more instances of Wodehouse using factual locations for his stories. Arundell Street vanished when they built this block of buildings around 1920.

**3.** *Walk on, crossing Rupert Street. A few yards beyond Rupert Street, on your left at 3-4 Coventry Street, is the door to what used to be the Café de Paris; it is now a restaurant, the Lio London.*

This was the location of the Café de Paris, better known to us as Mario's – yes, the Mario's we read of so often. When the first edition of this book was written, the Café de Paris was still going as a popular night-spot, though the clientele had changed over the years. Unfortunately, the Covid pandemic forced its closure in December 2020, after almost 100 years.

The Café de Paris was built originally in 1914 as the underground Elysée Restaurant, and the layout was based on the Palm Court of a famous liner, the *Lusitania*. In the 1920s and '30s, with the exception of the Embassy in Bond Street, it was the smartest nightclub in London, and the Prince of Wales

(later Duke of Windsor) came here for private lessons in the Charleston. There was an impressive double staircase that took you down to the dance floor, but if you were not in full evening dress (white tie and tails), you were relegated to tables on the balcony above it. This provided Wodehouse with the perfect opportunity for misunderstandings to arise between his heroes and heroines, when the heroine, up on the balcony, sees the hero dancing below with another woman. You will recall he always does so for perfectly innocent reasons which, of course, the heroine only discovers after she has broken their engagement.

Wodehouse featured Mario's in seven books, from *Ukridge* in 1924 to *Cocktail Time* over thirty years later; in *Bill the Conqueror*, he used it no fewer than six times. And who can forget Ronnie Fish's ambition to kill as many of the waiters as he could in *Summer Lightning*?

**4.** *Retrace your steps and turn right up Rupert Street, keeping on the left-hand side. Stop 10 yards short of the Blue Posts pub on the other side of the street.*

Rupert Street is mentioned in five Wodehouse books: *Not George Washington*; *The Girl on the Boat* (aka *Three Men and a Maid*); *The Adventures of Sally*; *Mulliner Nights*; and *Full Moon*, in which Gally Threepwood goes off to have lunch with a confidence trick man at the Pig & Whistle pub in Rupert Street. But the street's major importance is for the lodgings of Herbert Westbrook, the idle young man with big ideas who sponged on Wodehouse, swiped his clothes, pawned his banjo, and was perpetually unable to pay his debts, making him unmistakeably the major source of Stanley Featherstonhaugh Ukridge.

If you have read that very early Wodehouse book *Not George Washington* (1907), you will recall that the co-author was Herbert Westbrook. Narrated by two young men, the book contains so much reality that it is almost autobiographical. One narrator, Cloyster, is based on Wodehouse himself, and in the book he first meets the other young man, Julian Eversleigh, based on Westbrook, on the corner of the alley beside the Blue Posts pub. We are told that Eversleigh lives in the house beside the alley and that his landlord is a muffin baker called Mr Vancott. It will come as no surprise that the directory of 1907 shows there were only seven muffin bakers in central London, and one of them – Mr Forscutt, not Mr Vancott – had his business there. We are also told that Eversleigh/Westbrook had his rooms at the top of the house.

The significance of this is that Westbrook did live here, and it was up there, behind that small top window, on one evening in February 1905, that Bill Townend told Wodehouse and Westbrook the story of the disastrous chicken farming venture of an eccentric friend of his, Samuel Carrington Craxton. I have seen a photocopy of the letter from Townend to Wodehouse in which Townend remembered doing so in Westbrook's room in Rupert Street, and he recalled that both Westbrook and Wodehouse decided to write a story about it. And, just to confirm the date, I have a photocopy of a letter from Wodehouse to Townend written soon afterwards, in March 1905, in which Wodehouse says Westbrook was far too idle and would never do it! So – up there is where it all began: where Wodehouse got the plot for his first adult novel and where Stanley Featherstonhaugh Ukridge and his big ideas for making money originated.

**5.** *Walk down Rupert Court, the narrow alley beside the pub, turn right at the end, and after a few yards turn left into Lisle Street, then take the first right into Leicester Street. Walk down till you reach the posts in the middle of the road, then stop and look back at the restaurant called Slug & Lettuce.*

That peculiar ornate building was built about 1899 as the French Club, but from about 1928 to 1988, this was St John's Hospital for Skin Diseases. The hospital was originally set up elsewhere in 1863 by Dr John Laws Milton. He was an excellent dermatologist but also a bit of quack, and there were a series of financial scandals which left the hospital with a poor reputation. That is the reason why the pub that used to be located here was called The Crooked Surgeon. *(The pub closed a few years after the first edition was published. It is now the Slug & Lettuce, but that may change with the march of time.)*

**6.** *Walk down to Leicester Square in front of you and turn half-left to the railings round the garden directly in front of the Empire Casino.*

This enormous building was once the Empire Music Hall. Along with the Pelican Club and Romano's Restaurant (pronounced 'Roman Nose', not 'Romahno's'!), Leicester Square – especially the Empire – was the centre of Gally Threepwood's London. When you came back on leave from your five years in the Sudan, India, or Hong Kong, the old Empire, built in 1884, was where you always came – because there would always be somebody there you knew. It was famous, or notorious, for the Promenade which ran round the auditorium and had several bars along it where 'the ladies of the Empire', as they were known, would provide company for a lonely young man if he wanted it. They were discreet and well-behaved, which is why the Empire tolerated them, but in 1894 the new London County Council insisted on a screen being put up between the auditorium and the promenade. It lasted a week before being torn down by a party of Sandhurst cadets led by Officer Cadet Winston Churchill – his debut in public affairs.

The old music hall became a theatre later, and it closed in 1927. The last show was Fred and Adele Astaire's *Lady Be Good*, and the four Royal dukes – Wales, York, Gloucester, and Kent – were in the audience for the last night.

Look up there above the marquee. Can you see the enormous ornate archway behind it? That is the façade of the old music hall. Now look at the Queen's House to the right. That was built in 1897. Now look at the building in the same style, to the right of the Queen's House. And further along, you can see the same ornate, brash, confident, unrestrained Victorian style. If you wanted to have a successful restaurant/

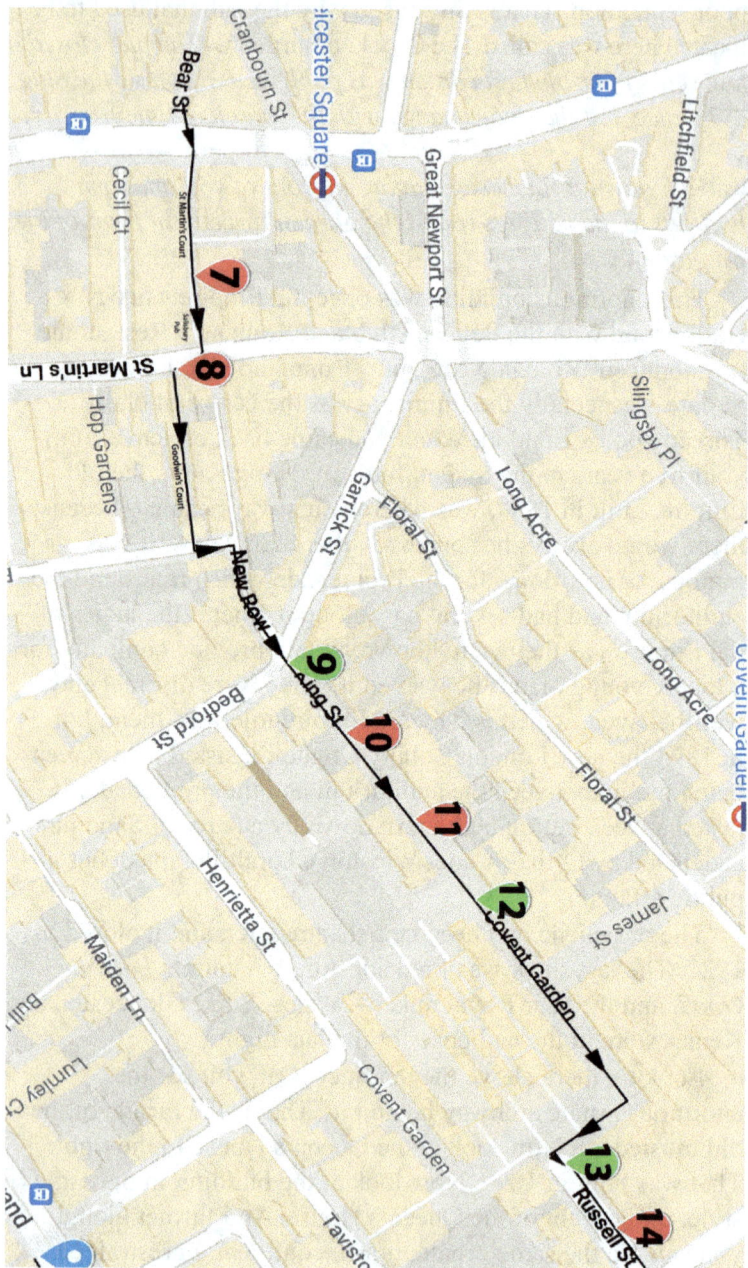

theatre/pub in Leicester Square, you had to look impressive. In the 1890s, Gally Threepwood's heyday, nearly all the buildings around the square looked like this.

The old Alhambra, which rivalled the Empire, was where the Odeon cinema is now, behind you on your right. That's where they have all those Royal Film premieres nowadays. The Alhambra (1850–1936) was where Leotard made his first appearance in the 1860s. He was the 'Daring young man on the flying trapeze, He flies though the air with the greatest of ease', and the tight-fitting costume worn by ballet dancers today is named after the costume he wore. The old Gardenia nightclub that Gally Threepwood mentioned frequently was at No. 29, beside the Alhambra

**7.** *With the Empire on your left, walk to the corner of the Square, turn half-right down Bear Street, and cross Charing Cross Road into St Martin's Court. Walk along the Court.*

On the wall of 'The Round Table' on the right is a plaque giving a history of the pub and mentioning the fight between the American Heenan and Sayers, the British champion. Heenan came over in 1860 and stayed here before the fight, which went on for 42 rounds. It was, effectively, the first world boxing championship, a bloody affair in every way, and it was eventually declared a draw. British and American fans have claimed victory for their countryman ever since.

At the end of St Martin's Court, on the right, is The Salisbury pub, one of the best examples of an 1890s pub, with gilt and cut/engraved glass everywhere.

**8.** *At the end of St Martin's Court, cross St Martin's Lane, turn right and, after a few yards, turn left into the narrow, easy-to-miss entrance of Goodwin's Court on the left. (Do NOT go along New Row!) A few yards along the Court, just before the first doorway (No. 56), there are some small windows in the old wall on your left.*

I can remember when there were bars on those windows. They were there because this was the old parish watch house, in the days before we had police stations. Each parish had beadles or watchmen who met here each evening before going out to keep the peace, and any drunks or baddies would be locked up in here overnight. I point this out now because we will soon be looking at London's oldest police station – the famous Bosher Street of Wodehouse's stories.

**9.** *Walk up Goodwin's Court, noting the plaque on the left-hand wall saying these houses were built in the 1690s. At the end of Goodwin's Court, turn left up Bedfordbury and then right on New Row. Keep the Tesco building on your right, cross Bedford Street, and stop on the corner on the other side. Turn around so you are looking back at Tesco.*

**a.** The street down here to your left is Bedford St. The large white building at No. 39, down there on the left-hand side, used to be home to *The Lady* magazine for nearly a century. I'd love to say it was the original of Aunt Dahlia's *Milady's Boudoir*, but I'm afraid I have nothing to support the idea.

**b.** Now, I am sure you remember the Cohen Brothers of Covent Garden. It was they who sold Wallace Chesney the Magic Plus-Fours and equipped Osbert Mulliner when he planned his escape to the Far East in 'The Ordeal of Osbert Mulliner'.

Wodehouse's readers knew he was referring to Moss Brothers, the country's biggest clothes-hire firm, who have been known as 'Mossbross' for over a century. 'Mossbross' were founded in 1851 and began hiring clothes in 1897 in the old building where Tesco is now. Wodehouse mentioned Moss Brothers as often as he did the Cohen Brothers, which puzzled me for years until I realised he called them Cohen Brothers when he was making fun of them and Moss Brothers when he referred to them seriously. Read the books again and you'll see what I mean.

Wodehouse didn't exaggerate their range of clothing. Until I got my own morning dress, I used to come here when I had a wedding to attend, and I always used to take the creaky old lift to the top of the building and then walk down through all the floors. I did so to enjoy looking at shelves piled high with every form of clothing and uniform you can imagine. There was one room devoted entirely to peers' robes with rows of shelves for the different coronets worn by dukes, earls, viscounts and the rest of them. It is believed that at least a third of the peers attending the Queen's coronation in 1953 were fitted out by Moss Brothers; Uncle Fred and Lord Emsworth returned their hired robes here after the Opening of Parliament in *Service with a Smile*. They had dress uniforms of every Army regiment, tropical clothing, arctic clothing, judge's robes, red tailcoats for fox-hunters – every form of uniform or dress worn by Englishmen anywhere in the world.

Wodehouse was right; they were all here.

**c**. That was until 29 January 1989, when they left the old building and moved across the road to No. 27 King Street on your right. *(Note: Sometime between 2012 and 2020, Moss Brothers left this location. As of 2023, it is a women's fashion store.)* With several branches all over London, Moss Bros. are still England's biggest hirer of dress suits and morning dress, but I regret to say you can't hire your ducal robes or coronet from them any more.

This building was, from 1808 to 1988, the headquarters of the Westminster Fire Insurance Company, whose impressive coat of arms is still up there on the wall. The portcullis is the badge of the city of Westminster, and the fleur-de-lys above it is there because they wanted to tell the world that George I's son, later George II, had given them his patronage when they were founded in 1717. No one knows why he did so, but since that was the year he had the tremendous row with his father, who banned him from all Court ceremonies, perhaps they provided the Prince with a tactful loan or some free fire insurance on his house in Leicester Square. The actor David

*(Photo courtesy of Robert Bruce)*

Garrick lodged here in 1748, in the building on the site before this one.

**10.** *Walk along the right-hand side of King Street towards Covent Garden and pause opposite No. 31 on the other side of the road. (As of 2023, the building houses Floral Court.)*

The blue plaque over there marks the birthplace and home of Thomas Arne. He was the chap who wrote 'Rule Britannia'.

**11.** *Walk on till you are opposite no 37.*

Across the road, Nos. 34–39 used to have – and maybe some still do – the first mahogany doors in England. Around 1720, a Dr Gibbons of King Street was presented with some baulks of timber by his brother, a naval captain. His brother had come across this remarkably heavy, dense wood in the West Indies, and the ship's carpenter had been unable to do anything with it. His chisels simply weren't good enough to work the unusual timber. Dr Gibbons's cabinet-maker was not able to do anything with them either, so the doctor simply had them made into doors for his house and those of his neighbours. My sources said that it was not until some ten years later that the first piece of mahogany furniture was made in England for – guess who – Dr Gibbons of King Street!

Behind us, at no. 6 King Street, was the site of the Essex Serpent pub, the only one by that name in London. This legendary creature, known as a cockatrice, killed people just by looking at them. The serpent was, allegedly, killed by a knight who polished his armour so brightly that the serpent died when it saw its own reflection. Whatever the serpent or cockatrice was, we know the legend goes back to the twelfth century – and there had been a pub here in King Street by this name since at least 1676. *(But no longer, alas. The Essex Serpent closed in February 2014.)*

**12.** *Into Covent Garden. Go a few yards beyond the big building on your left (43 King St) with two columns at its entrance and stop just inside the first wooden barrier.*

**a.** This is England's first purpose-built town square, designed and laid out by Inigo Jones in the 1630s on ground owned by the Earls of Bedford, who had been given it by Henry VIII. The Bedfords held onto it till 1914. It is a splendid example of developers giving something one name and Londoners giving it another.

Inigo Jones had been to Livorno, Italy, saw a lovely piazza there, and copied it here – London's first town square. When the job was done, Jones asked everybody to come and admire his superb 'piazza' – the Italian name for what we call a square and the French call a 'place' (e.g., Place de la Concorde. The trouble was that Londoners hadn't seen a square or 'place' or piazza before – hence the subsequent confusion lasting over 350 years. Londoners saw an open space which they reckoned was, well, just an open space, and the more Inigo Jones banged on about this weird piazza thing, the more Londoners reckoned the piazza must be those funny buildings round this side of the square with arcades underneath them, which were also new to this country. That is why the arcade on the northern side, just there in front of you, is still, incorrectly, called The Piazza – and the Square doesn't have a name to this day. It is still just Covent Garden, because this had been the vegetable garden for the Westminster Convent until around 1540 – and Londoners saw no reason to call it anything else, no matter what Inigo Jones said.

In passing, 'Piazza' became the smart name for London children for the next thirty years. The parish registers of the time are full of little Piazza Browns, Piazza Robinsons, and Piazza Smiths.

**b.** Orford House (43 King St), the big house on northern side where the left-hand end of the piazza ends (as you look at it), is the only building left from the days when Covent Garden was a smart residential area. In 1892, when Gally Threepwood's beloved Pelican Club collapsed in a welter of writs, lawsuits, and bankruptcy orders, one half of the membership went off and founded the Eccentric Club. The other half came here and founded the National Sporting Club in this big building. Known as the NSC, it made boxing respectable. This was where Battling Billson fought Alf Todd in 'The Return of Battling Billson', where Freddie Threepwood met George Emerson in *Something Fresh*, and where Joe Bevan fought in *The White Feather*. Wodehouse's accurate description of it indicates he almost certainly attended boxing evenings here. A blue plaque on the building identifies it as the site of the NSC.

**c.** St Paul's church, down the slope behind you, is a bit severe in style, but only because the Earl of Bedford didn't want the expense of building a big church and told Inigo Jones back in 1635 that it could look like a barn. Jones replied: "I will build you the handsomest barn in Christendom." Hence the severe, non-ornamented building you see. It was burned down but re-built to the same design. If you wonder why this end is blank, it is because Jones originally intended it to be the main door into the church. But then William Laud, Archbishop of Canterbury (1633–45), realised what was going on and said "Oy! You can't do that there 'ere", and made sure Jones changed it. Anglican churches have their altars at the east end of the church, not the west, so Jones had to close up the vast entrance, move the altar up to this end and put the main door down at the other (west) end. The clock in the pediment above it has a face coloured the blue of the sky and the figures the gold of the stars because Henry VIII decreed back in 1540 or thereabouts that church clocks should be painted that way. The clock of St Martin-in-the-Field in Trafalgar Square is the same.

**d.** Samuel Pepys saw the first Punch and Judy show in England here in 1662, as the notice on the church portico tells us. And you will recall that in George Bernard Shaw's play *Pygmalion* (or the musical *My Fair Lady*), Professor Higgins first met Eliza Doolittle under that portico.

Covent Garden was the central fruit and vegetable market for London and the Home Counties from about 1680 till they moved down to Nine Elms in 1973. The market buildings in the centre date from 1830, and as Wodehouse told us and I can confirm, the area around here, where Sippy Sipperley and Aunt Dahlia had their editorial offices, always seemed to have cabbage leaves blowing everywhere. Since the market began about midnight and went on till about 8 in the morning, they had a special licensing hours for the pubs here – but you were not allowed to buy a drink unless you could show you had business in the market. I remember once in the Army, back in 1953 or so, finding myself here at 2 in the morning and dying for a drink. I asked a stallholder what to do and he said, "Here, you are. Buy an apple." I did so, and walked in the pub proudly carrying my purchase – and saw a dozen or so other soldiers and late travellers each displaying a carrot, an apple, or a beetroot alongside their glass of beer.

**e.** Down at the lower end of Covent Garden, beyond the church, is Henrietta Street. Jane Austen stayed there with her brother in 1813 at No. 10 Henrietta Street. In direct contrast to Miss Austen's genteel world, the only mention of Henrietta Street in Wodehouse is in *Love Among the Chickens*. Corky, the narrator, described Ukridge as the sort of man who invites you to dinner, has to borrow the money from you to pay for it, and then gets you involved in a row in Covent Garden that ends up with the pair of you being chased along Henrietta Street by a crowd of infuriated costermongers. Very different from the world of Miss Austen.

**13.** *Continue the Walk along this side of the Market building, turn right at the end and then left into Russell Street, pausing on the corner.*

In *Not George Washington*, the narrator and his friends leave a Covent Garden dress ball in the Opera House on your left at dawn and come up Russell Street to the Hummums Hotel for breakfast. The old Hummums Hotel stood just here on your right on the corner of Russell Street and the Market (at 11-12 Russell St; Tutton's is there now). Named after the first Turkish baths in England that were built here around 1670, the Hummums Hotel was demolished around 1930.

**14.** *Walk along the left-hand side of Russell Street, pausing opposite No. 8.*

At No. 8 you can see a plaque on the wall pointing out that this was the home of Davies the bookseller, where Boswell was introduced to Dr Johnson on 16 May 1763. It was a favourite spot for literary men to gather – one major attraction being Mrs Davies, the bookshop owner's beautiful wife.

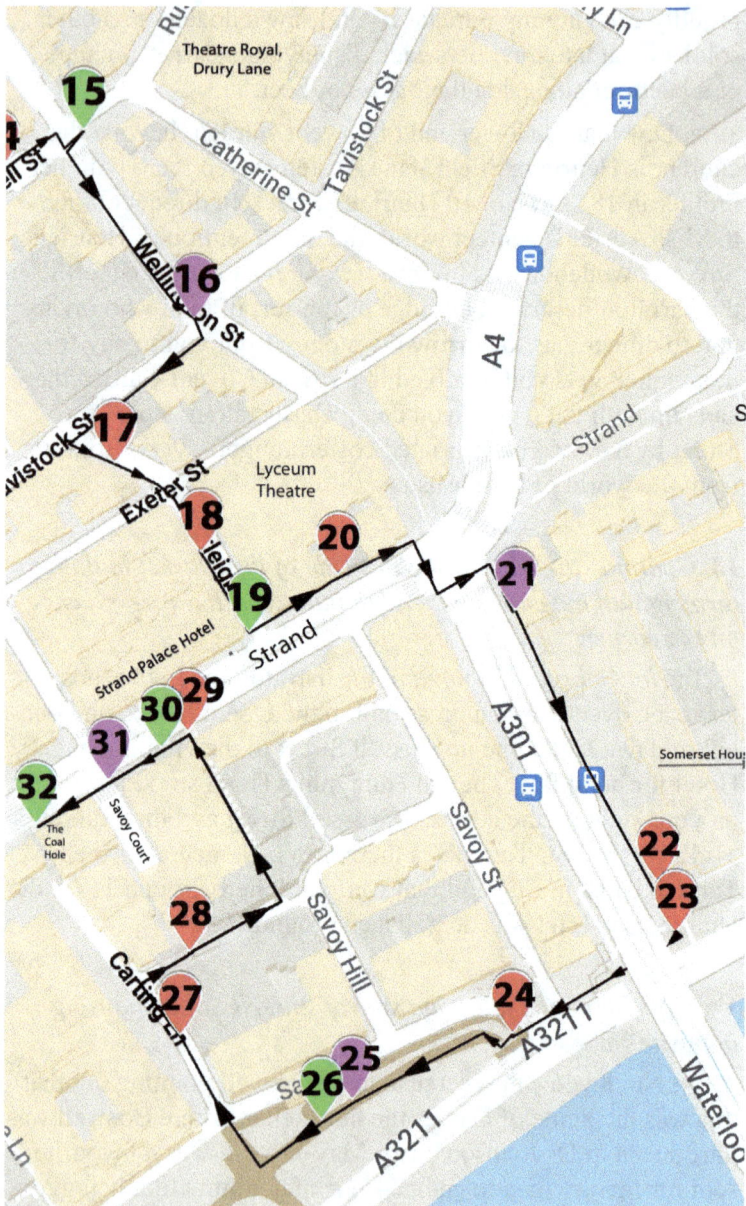

**15.** *At the junction with Bow Street, cross over to the right-hand side of Russell Street so you can then use the zebra crossing to get to the other side of Wellington Street. Cross over, stop on the corner and turn round to look up Bow Street (which continues from Wellington St).*

**a.** At the far end, up there on the left, are the pillars of the main entrance of the Royal Opera House, which date from 1809, though the rest of the theatre has twice been destroyed by fire since then. The grey building on the other side of the road is, or was until July 2006, the Bow Street police court.

It was the oldest police court in the country. It began around 1740 and became well known through the efficiency of the magistrate Henry Fielding, the famous novelist, and his Bow Street Runners, London's first organised police force. We know it better as Bosher Street, where Bertie Wooster was fined five pounds in the short story 'Without the Option' and poor old Sippy Sipperley was given thirty days under the name Leon Trotzky. It was in Bosher Street that Ronnie Fish was fined a fiver for trying to kill the waiters in Mario's in *Summer Lightning*. In *Cocktail Time* later, Cosmo Wisdom got fourteen days at Bosher Street when a policeman objected strongly to his helmet being stolen.

**b.** Turn to the right and ahead of you, half-right, you can see the Theatre Royal, Drury Lane (corner of Russell Street and Catherine Street). The Theatre Royal, Drury Lane, is London's oldest theatre. The first one on this site was built in 1663, and Samuel Pepys saw Nell Gwynn here. The present building on the site is the fourth and was opened in 1819 with a Prologue written by Lord Byron. The theatre has several ghosts, the best known of which, 'The Man In Grey', has been seen so often over the years that people don't even report it any more. And if you ask why it is called The Theatre Royal, Drury Lane, when the entrance has always been on Catherine Street, I have been unable to find an answer in twenty years. Drury Lane, the home of the heroic Gladys in 'Lord Emsworth and the Girl Friend', is the street down at the far end of the theatre.

**16.** *Go back over the zebra crossing, then turn left down Wellington Street and stay on the right-hand side. Stop at the corner of Tavistock Street, which crosses Wellington Street.*

Somewhere along Wellington Street, where we are now, was a scruffy, disreputable Bohemian club known as the Yorick. Wodehouse joined it in 1903 and wrote about it in *Not George Washington*, but I haven't been able to find out where it was. You can't win them all. But there is something to note here. Look to your left, along Tavistock Street. Look three houses along on the right-hand side and then up at the roof line. See that white panel up there just under the roof? You can't read it from here but it says 'YORK STREET 1636'. It is London's oldest street sign, and nobody knows why it is still there – but, thank heaven, it is.

Just across the road from you is the narrow angle of the building at the Tavistock St–Wellington St junction. A few feet to the right of the corner is the plaque marking the office where Charles Dickens edited his magazine *All The Year Round* from 1859 to 1870.

**17.** *Turn right into Tavistock Street, then take the first left down into Burleigh Street. Cross over to walk down the right-hand side. Ten yards down, on your left, is the remarkable Victorian Gothic clergy house for St Paul's, Covent Garden.*

If you know your Victorian architects and that building seems familiar, you are right. That was the clergy house for the church up in Covent Garden, built by Butterfield in 1859. He was the chap who built Keble College in Oxford and a leading exponent of the Victorian Gothic building style you see here. When in doubt, use brick, but employ as many different colours of bricks and patterns of bricklaying as you can think of.

**18.** *Continue down Burleigh Street towards the Strand, crossing over Exeter Street. About twenty yards further on, across the road, is a big wall with three panels on it. They are marked Terry, Stoker, and Irving.*

See those three names over there? Terry, Stoker, and Irving? That is the re-built back of the Lyceum Theatre, where Ellen

Terry and Henry Irving dominated the English stage for thirty years at the end of the nineteenth century. Irving (1838–1905) was the man who revolutionised British acting – and he liked realism. There was the famous occasion when he was rehearsing Shakespeare's *The Tempest*. He was trying to get the stage manager to get his sound effects the way Irving wanted, but the poor chap couldn't do it. Irving had stopped the rehearsal to tell him yet again what he wanted was a clap of thunder that really sounded like a clap of thunder. Just as he paused for breath, a storm broke overhead with a clap of thunder that shook the entire theatre. Irving was delighted: "Splendid! Superb! Do it just that way tonight!"

And Stoker? He was Bram Stoker, Irving's friend and business manager, who did some writing in his spare time and gave us *Dracula* in 1897.

**19.** *At the bottom of Burleigh Street, pause at the right corner.*

The building here on the right is now the Strand Palace Hotel. The corner we are on was the site of *The Globe* evening paper for whom Wodehouse started working in 1901 and whose staff he joined in 1903.

**20.** *Turn left and continue along the Strand until you reach the Lyceum Tavern on the left.*

Many years ago, I learned that this tavern used to have a private entrance from the back of the Lyceum Theatre, so actors could pop in for a quick drink in costume. As late as November 2006, I called in and found an old boy at the bar who confirmed the story and showed me the theatre fire exit that faces the back entrance of the pub, which used to be The Samuel Beazley. Beazley was the architect who built the Lyceum Theatre, not once but twice. His first 1816 version was destroyed by fire in 1834, so he built it again. He was well-known for his dissolute ways, drinking and wenching and so on, and for many years there was a plaque on the wall of the pub, allegedly copying his tombstone. It read:

> Here lies Samuel Beazley.
> He lived fast and died easily.

**21.** *Continue to the set of lights and cross to the other side of the Strand. Turn left again and cross over to the far side of Lancaster Place. Walk a few yards towards the river to clear the busy corner, then turn round and look back.*

**a.** From here you can see the Lyceum Tavern over to the left. Look to the right of the tavern, up Wellington Street, and you can see the magnificent pillars of the Lyceum Theatre. Though the theatre has been altered considerably, that portico is unchanged since Beazley built it in 1834. This was the theatre where Henry Irving dominated the theatrical world from 1870 till his death in 1905.

**b.** Look slightly right. Across the road from the Lyceum, the narrow building pointing towards you, separating Wellington Street from the Aldwych, was the site of the old Gaiety Theatre, built in 1868 and demolished in 1903. *(See Appendix 2.)* It then became the office of the old *Morning Post* newspaper, and it was from here that Churchill published the *British Gazette* during the General Strike of 1926. It is a hotel now, and if you have coffee or a drink there, the room downstairs is the old machine room where Churchill used to read the paper as it came off the presses.

Across from the upper corner of the Aldwych, on the right before the India House/Bush House block, is the site of second Gaiety Theatre, opened in 1903, closed in 1939, and demolished in 1956. It was there that PGW got the job of extra lyric-writer in 1907. At the age of 26, he was working in the most famous musical comedy theatre in the world. This was where he came into contact with the Gaiety Girls, whose marriages into the aristocracy provided the newspapers of the day with sensational headlines and gave novelists, including Wodehouse, fruitful material for the next forty years. Ronnie Fish and the family opposition when he wanted to marry Sue Brown was just one example.

**c.** I should point out that we are now standing on land owned by the Duchy of Lancaster. It is not significant nowadays, but it used to be quite important. Back in the fourteenth century, the Duchy of Lancaster was given to John of Gaunt and his successors. There are now several bits of

England owned by the Duchy, one of which is the parish of the Savoy in London, where we now are. Later, the successors of John of Gaunt became kings of England, which means the Queen is also Duke of Lancaster, and in Lancashire you do not toast 'The Queen', you drink to 'The Duke of Lancaster'. That is harmless enough but the legal complications of the Duchy's rights and privileges – were people living here subject to Lancashire taxes or London taxes and that sort of thing – resulted in George III having to bring an action against himself as Duke of Lancaster to find out what the legal position was. We shall see the Duchy boundary in a few minutes.

**22.** *Walk down the left-hand side of Lancaster Place with Somerset House on your left, till you reach the steps going down to the Embankment. Pause when you are in front of Somerset House.*

**a.** The splendid building on your left, Somerset House, was built in 1775 and was once home to many Government departments. It was best known for holding all the wills of people who had died in England and Wales. I spent a good six months of lunchtimes in here in 1976, checking through the wills of Wodehouse's 35 aunts and uncles and his innumerable cousins and in-laws. In those days it cost only 25 pence to look at a will, and they brought it to you in an enormous hand-written volume inside fifteen minutes. Now all the wills have been moved elsewhere, and they charge £5 a go. Scandalous! (*Amazingly, the cost has gone down to £1.50 online. –EWM*)

**b.** That terrace on your left used to overhang the river, and the arches where the boats came in carrying supplies are still down there. The terrace was closed to the public from 1775 till sometime in the early 2000s, and the little wooden bridge leading to it from the road here is very new. To be allowed to walk on the terrace used to be a privilege restricted to the civil servants who worked here, and when the female novelist George Eliot used to meet the philosopher and philanthropist Herbert Spencer in the 1850s and walk up and down here, engaged in deep philosophical discussion, it was exceptional enough to be noted by every diarist of the time.

**23.** *Go down the steps beside you to the Embankment. At the bottom of the steps, on the right, is the badge (three lions) marking the boundary of the Duchy of Lancaster.*

This badge here, of the Duchy of Lancaster, means we are now outside the Duchy, though we return to it again as we turn right here under the bridge.


**24.** *Turn right under the bridge and cross over to the beginning of Embankment Gardens, (the entrance is five yards along on the river side). Stop just before you turn right into the gardens and look at the base of the big street lamp beside you.*

Look at that badge. It says London County Council 1900 and shows Britannia holding a shield in either hand. It marks two very significant events in London's history. The London County Council, which governed what we call Greater London today, did not exist till 1888, and the City of Westminster, i.e. the bit of London west of the old City of London, did not exist till 1900. The old City of London was very jealous of its ancient privileges, and it needed a tremendous effort of goodwill to acknowledge the rival City of Westminster in 1900. These lamps along the Embankment here were the first project on which the two cities co-operated under the control of the London County Council – or so the London County Council liked to think. That is why the LCC is shown here as the authority figure represented by Britannia shown holding the two shields, like a mother controlling two children. The shield with a cross and a dagger is the City of London badge; the portcullis is the Westminster badge, and I believe these Embankment lampposts are the only places where you will see these two badges together. I don't know whether Westminster or the City of London ever agreed with this badge. I have an idea they probably didn't because it was never authorised by anybody, not even by the members of the LCC! They didn't get their official badge till 1914 and that was a very different one comprising three alternate wavy lines with a cross, a lion and a tower on top.

**25.** *Enter the path that goes into the Gardens, turn left, and walk along till you come to the memorial to Arthur Sullivan on your left.*

This is where officialdom got things right for a change. Sullivan's memorial is here, and Gilbert's is about fifty yards away in front of us on the Embankment, because officialdom realised the whole world associated Gilbert & Sullivan with the Savoy Theatre and Savoy Hotel, which their manager, D'Oyly Carte, built with the profits from their comic operas. And the Savoy Hotel is this enormous building rising up on our right now.

The Savoy Hotel features often in Wodehouse, probably because they provided after-theatre suppers, which many restaurants wouldn't do. The Savoy was always popular with theatre folk, and just about everybody who was anybody in the theatre stayed here, including Gigli, Caruso, Sarah Bernhardt, and Dame Nellie Melba; the peach Melba and Melba toast were both created here and named in her honour.

Way up there above us, the roof of the Savoy has seen many of London's best publicity stunts. Fred Astaire danced up there for the Press; Walter Hagen, the American golfer, started the custom, followed by many golfers later, of practising his driving up there, hitting balls into the Thames; and, most incongruous of all, when Jascha Heifetz (1901–87), the greatest violinist of the 20th century, stayed here in the 1930s, the Scottish comedian and singer Sir Harry Lauder gave him bagpipe lessons up there.

Now, let's talk about fly-fishing. In that sport you cast out a line with a small hook on the end decorated to look like a fly of some sort. Most beginners tend to throttle themselves or get the hook entangled with every bush within thirty yards before they learn to do it properly. The thing about fly-fishing is that you do not have any weight on the fishing line and just have to work with the line itself. And that means that casting a line any distance is very difficult.

Back in 1953, two Americans, both fly-fishers, were over in London to see the Coronation and were staying at the Savoy. One day they looked up at the roof up there and wondered –

was it possible to cast a fly from all the way up there over these trees into the River Thames behind us? They went to Hardy's, the fishing-tackle people, and Hardy's knew just the right man: Mr Esmond Drury. He was reluctant to do it because he had no head for heights but eventually agreed. Securely fastened to some solid object, very early on a Sunday morning with little traffic along the Embankment – and with the co-operation of a London policeman down here on the road – Mr Drury proved it is possible to cast a fly from up there into the Thames.

**26.** *Move on a few yards till you are in line with the Savoy Hotel River entrance. On your right is a small memorial. It is a small flower stand on a plinth with an orrery/sundial device.*

This memorial commemorates the three members of the D'Oyly Carte family who owned/managed the Savoy: Richard (the Gilbert & Sullivan impresario), who built the theatre in 1881 and the hotel in 1889; his son Rupert, who became chairman of the Savoy in 1901 after his father; and Dame Bridget, Rupert's daughter. We know Rupert D'Oyly Carte better as the original of Rupert Psmith, as Wodehouse always admitted. Carte was at Winchester with a cousin of Wodehouse's, and it was he who told Wodehouse of

the tall, languid schoolboy who, when a master said offhandedly, "How are you, Carte?", replied "Sir, I grow thinnah and thinnah."

**27.** *About fifteen yards beyond the Carte memorial, turn right and out of the gardens to the bottom of Carting Lane, which runs steeply uphill. On the left-hand side of the lane, there is a modern lamppost on the corner, but about fifteen yards beyond that, up the lane ahead of you, is a lamp with a very thick column and a gas lamp that is always alight. It is well worth a look.*

This is the famous – yes, it is famous – 'sewer gas lamp' patented by Webb's in 1879 to run off gases from the sewers. I believe it is the only one left in London, though Whitley Bay in the northeast coast is said to have a dozen or so. The sewer under here is probably a very old one, carrying sewage and waste from the Strand up there down to the river which, until 1874, came up to the bottom of the lane here. Despite its name, the gas lamp does not nowadays actually burn sewer gas. It is kept burning, night and day, to draw the gases up out of the sewer and into the open air where they are harmless.

**28.** *Walk up the lane, take the first right, with the back of the Savoy Theatre above you, and walk along the roadway to the right under the hotel. About fifteen yards along, stop and listen.*

Behind the louvres on your left, you can hear a dull roar. This is now the Savoy's air-conditioning system. It is also the oldest electric power station in England, if not the world, since D'Oyly Carte installed it to provide the hotel with electric light back in 1889. And there is a splendid story about it.

In 1945/6, the Government working party tasked with nationalising the electrical industry in the UK met in an office in the Savoy. They beavered away here for months, checking, listing all the electricity firms in the UK, finishing their work and publishing their report, and they were about to depart when, in a moment W.S. Gilbert could have written himself, the Savoy presented them with a bill for the electricity they had used. They had nationalised every electricity supplier in the UK – except one. With all their hard work and exhaustive inquiries, the Board had omitted to list the Savoy power station beside us.

**29.** *Continue up the road. Near the end, take the steps up on your left, Savoy Buildings. As you reach the Strand at the top of the alley, you pass the ornate plaque recording Fountain Court and the site of the original Coal Hole pub.*

For some reason, the plaque does not mention William Blake, the painter and poet who wrote the hymn 'Jerusalem' and died here in 1827.

**30.** *Turn left at the top, go along, and pause outside 100 Strand, the site of Simpson's in the Strand.*

Wodehouse had a very high opinion of Simpson's and referred to it at least five times in his books: *Psmith in the City*, *Something Fresh*, *Big Money*, *If I Were You*, and *Cocktail Time*. Many felt it served the best beef in Britain, and until it closed during the Covid pandemic, the downstairs dining

room remained unchanged from the time PGW knew it more than a century ago. When Aline Peters lunched here with George Emerson in *Something Fresh*, we know they dined upstairs because ladies were not allowed in the down-stairs dining room till October 1983. That was when Parliament made such segregation illegal, and City gentlemen were no longer able to lunch in peace, safe from the temptation of a well-turned ankle or a sidelong roguish smile. I also have to tell you that the splendid old rule of eating as much as you liked for five shillings (25 pence (60 cents US in 2009, 30 cents in 2023) stopped with the start of the World War in 1914.

(*Note: In 2023, Simpson's furniture and fixtures were sold at auction. There are plans to reopen in grand style, though its classic look will be much missed, and I just know Norman would have been muttering about the evils of change. –EWM*)

**31.** *Continue down the Strand until you come to Savoy Court. Do not cross over but turn down the left-hand side for five yards or so to get away from the noisy street.*

**a.** This is the Savoy Hotel with, above the entrance, the chromium statue of Peter of Savoy (1203–68), who built the first palace of Savoy on this site. He was uncle to Eleanor of Provence, who married Henry III, and as her guardian he came along with her to see what he could pick up in the way of jobs around the Court, a bit of land here and there and a lot of marriage-broking. That sort of thing.

D'Oyly Carte built the hotel here on the American model in 1889 and said he wanted seventy bathrooms. This was considered extraordinary at the time; Brown's Hotel and Claridge's worked on the basis of one bathroom for every hundred guests, and the Savoy architect was convinced D'Oyly Carte was joking. It is recorded that he asked Carte: "Are you building a hotel or an aquarium?"

In *A Gentleman of Leisure*, Wodehouse had Jimmy Pitt staying in Savoy Mansions down here on the left, and mentioned the Savoy often as somewhere the hero could take the heroine for a late supper after the theatre.

**b.** There are three things to notice here. The first is that it is the only place in the UK where cars drive on the right. This is not to make Americans feel at home, but for a practical reason. Taxis bringing people to the theatre down there at the right-hand corner can drop them off there and then pick up anyone at the hotel wanting a taxi. If the normal rules applied, taxis would back up from the theatre entrance across the front of the hotel and jam everything up. The Savoy needed to get an Act of Parliament to change the rules, but they did it. When my wife Elin and I first tried out this Walk, we saw a young taxi-driver forgetting where he was and driving on the left. He was hooted at very sharply by his colleagues.

The second thing to notice is the chromium plaques on the walls down either side. These recount the site's history; I wish more hotels or offices were equally informative. Years ago, they were all taken down for cleaning or refurbishing or something and then replaced – but in the wrong order! Luckily for the Savoy, a Nosey Parker from the Ministry of Defence who spent his lunchtimes walking around London keeping an eye on things like this came along and pointed it out – but none of the people I spoke to thought it was important. I'd been in the Ministry long enough to learn how to work these things and promptly wrote a letter to the manager, enclosing a copy of the letter I proposed to send to the Press, pointing out how a hotel like the Savoy should know better. It worked like a charm – the plaques were all replaced in the right order within a week. Someone has to keep an eye on these things.

Third, the Savoy Theatre is down on the right-hand side. When it was built in 1881, crowds gathered every night to try and get tickets for the Gilbert & Sullivan operettas, which were as wildly popular then as modern concerts are now. And because D'Oyly Carte did not want the patrons of his new hotel to be upset by the theatre crowds outside, he brought in heavies to keep the crowds in order and make them line up one behind the other, in an orderly way – and now you know where Britain saw its first organised queuing system.

**32.** *Cross the Savoy Court, and after a few feet, stop outside the Coal Hole.*

**a.** Along with The Shakespeare pub by Victoria Station, The White Hart at Barnes, and the Cheshire Cheese, the Coal Hole is one of the four London pubs Wodehouse mentioned that are still on the same site. It was here that Corcoran and Ukridge retired for a drink in the short story 'The Debut of Battling Billson'. As we saw just now, the original Coal Hole was some forty yards behind us, but when they built the Savoy Hotel and got rid of the old pub, someone decided to keep the name going. Thomas Edward Colcutt, the architect who built the hotel, built this Coal Hole in 1904.

**b.** Across the Strand is Southampton Street. W.S. Gilbert, for whom Wodehouse had a tremendous admiration, was born at No. 17. Do you see the big, ornate clock sticking out of the wall on the right-hand side? From 1891 to 1950, that building contained the offices of *The Strand* magazine in which so many Wodehouse stories appeared. It also contained the offices of *The Captain* and *Tit-Bits* magazines; if you know your Wodehouse, you will recall that he sold his first jokes to *Tit-*

*Bits* and made his name with his school stories in *The Captain*. At the top of the street, Henrietta Street runs off to the left – and along there were the offices of *Pearson's Magazine*, which also took a lot of Wodehouse's early work.

**c.** Back to Gally Threepwood for a moment: Romano's (pronounced 'Roman Nose') was along there to the left at 399 the Strand, forty yards along on the other side. It is now the Stanley Gibbons stamp shop. They pulled the old building down in the 1950s, but if you stand on the pavement outside, you can still win the bet that you can see the Law Courts clock way, way down there to the right, despite the two churches that stand in the way (though only in winter since they planted trees whose leaves now obscure the clock in summer).

*Proof positive that the Law Courts clock can be seen from where Romano's once stood in the Strand – in wintertime, anyway!. (Thanks to Robert Bruce)*

On the first Wodehouse Walk, when we arrive at the junction of Hay's Mews and Charles Street, beside the Footman pub, I always announce solemnly that we are at the heart of Bertie Wooster's Mayfair. Well, with Romano's over there on the left, the *Globe* offices just down there to the right where the Strand Palace Hotel is now, and *Tit-Bits*, *The Captain*, *The Strand*, and *Pearson's* just over there, I reckon we are now at the heart of Wodehouse's early London, the London of Gally Threepwood and Stanley Ukridge.

That's the end of this Walk, so I suggest a drink here in the Coal Hole, where Ukridge and Corky had one in 'The Debut of Battling Billson' more than eighty years ago.

# Walk 3

## Valley Fields:
## A Wodehouse Walk in Dulwich

### Introduction

**P.G.** Wodehouse entered Dulwich College in April 1894 at the age of 13½ and left it in July 1900. He revisited it constantly and held the College in great affection to the end of his long life. Many commentators have been puzzled by, and slightly dismissive of, his attachment to the College because they do not appreciate that it was his real boyhood home. His father was a magistrate in Hong Kong, and home leave was only granted every five years, which meant that Wodehouse spent most of his childhood being brought up by aunts and uncles in England. Dulwich was the first fixed base in his life; it gave him the stability and routine every young person needs.

Dulwich also gave Wodehouse the background for his early school stories, and he reinforced this with frequent visits back to the school over the next four or five years, noting events and incidents there with the comment: "Use in school story."

The first mention of Dulwich under its own name is in *Psmith in the City* (1910), but we do not hear of it again for fifteen years until *Sam the Sudden* (1925). In the early 1920s, Wodehouse came back from America to live in London, and he resumed his regular visits here to watch the College Rugger team. This time he saw it not as a setting for his school stories but as an ideal location for his light novels. He was living in Mayfair then, but the quiet orderliness and greenery of Dulwich/'Valley Fields' – like that of Remsenburg, Long Island, later – was where he was happiest.

In the introduction to the 1972 edition of *Sam the Sudden*, Wodehouse wrote: "It was the first thing of mine where the action took place in the delectable suburb of Valley Fields, a thin disguise for the Dulwich where so many of my happiest

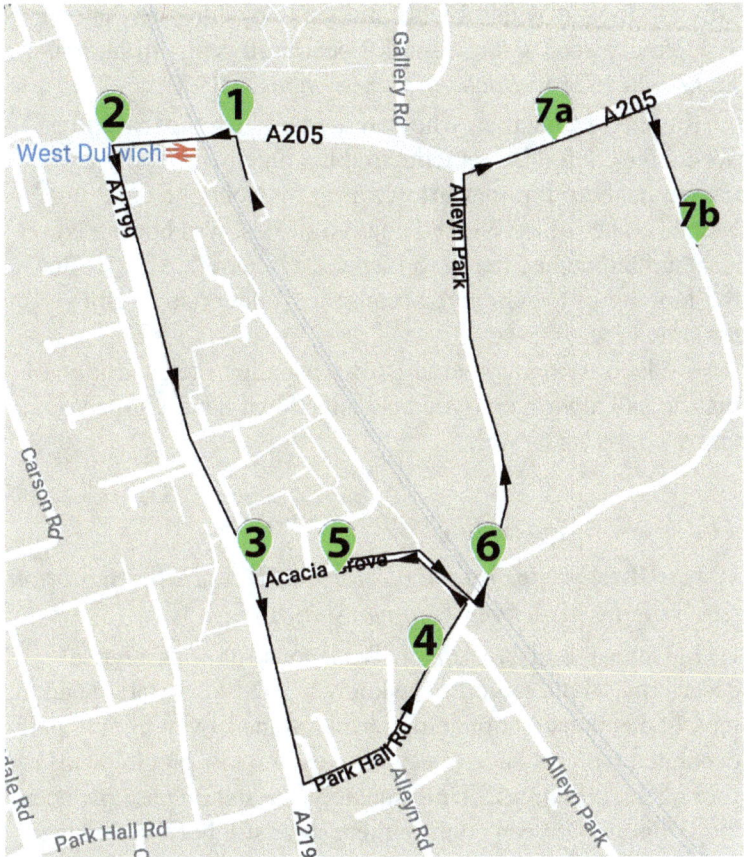

hours have been spent. In the course of a longish life I have flitted about a bit. I have had homes in Mayfair, in Park Avenue, New York, in Beverly Hills, California, and other posh localities, but I have always been a suburbanite at heart, and it is when I get a plot calling for a suburban setting that I really roll up my sleeves and give of my best."

Several Wodehouse characters were given addresses in Dulwich, including Albert Peasemarch (*Cocktail Time*), Spink's mother (*Spring Fever*), and Mrs Maudie Wilberforce ('Indian Summer of an Uncle'). And who can forget that when Bertie was apprehended by the police, it was the work of a moment for him to assume the identity of Eustace H. Plimsoll, The Laburnums, Alleyn Road, West Dulwich? But we are going to look at Valley Fields and the two addresses that Wodehouse used and re-used for nearly 50 years, from *Sam the Sudden* in 1925 to *Bachelors Anonymous* in 1973.

Raymond Chandler, who entered Dulwich the term after Wodehouse left, also remembered his time here fondly and named his hero Philip Marlowe after his School House. Ngaio Marsh, writer of excellent detective stories, was born in New Zealand but named her hero Inspector Roderick Alleyn after the founder of the College because her father had so enjoyed his time here.

Wodehouse remembered Dulwich/Valley Fields fondly all his life and always enjoyed his visits down here. I hope you enjoy your visit as well.


## *The Walk*  *(Map on page 89)*

*1. This Walk begins on the platform of West Dulwich Station (arriving by train from Victoria Station).*

In Chapter 5 of *Big Money*, Wodehouse gave us a lyrical description of the station as he knew it: "The very station had the look of a country station. Grass banks sloped away from it, gaily decorated with cabbages, beets, and even roses. Not to mention four distinct beehives." Unfortunately, the station has now been modernised, but I can confirm there were still beehives on the railway banking when I first came here in the 1970s.

As you come down the steps of the Down platform (trains from London) and walk down the long ramp to the street, the College grounds are on your right. When Wodehouse came down to watch the Dulwich Rugger team playing, that was the obvious direction for him to take, and it took me a long time to find out why he did not do so. The reason is that the school matches began at 2 or 2.15 p.m., and if Wodehouse wanted to have lunch, he had to leave his London house about noon, travel down here, have a beer and some bread and cheese in the Alleyn's Head pub, and then go and watch the College team doing their stuff. This walk follows the circuitous route he took and also retraces the steps of Lord Biskerton in *Big Money* when he comes to Valley Fields to escape his creditors.

Turn left as you come out of the station, and you pass by a newspaper kiosk. *(Note: Unable to confirm if the kiosk is still there in 2023. –EWM)* In his letter to Bill Townend of 28 April 1925 (*Performing Flea*), Wodehouse wrote: "Do you remember when we used to stand outside the bookstall at Dulwich station on the first of the month, waiting for Stanhope to open it so we could get the new Strand with the latest instalment of Rodney Stone?"

Walk under the railway bridge, noting the old-fashioned signpost on the other side of the road with a hand directing you to West Norwood. I have been unable to ascertain why Dulwich has retained these, but they make a delightful contrast to today's standard road signs.

**2.** *Stop at the junction of Croxted Road and Thurlow Park Road (A205).*

The building immediately on your left as you approach the corner occupies the site of what was 62 Croxted Road. This is where Wodehouse's parents took a house for some months in 1895 when his father retired from the Hong Kong Civil Service. Wodehouse used it to create the conjoined Mon Repos and San Rafael, Burberry Road, of *Sam the Sudden*; Mon Repos, Burberry Road, of *Company for Henry*; Restharrow, Croxley Road, of *Do Butlers Burgle Banks?*; 11 Croxted Road of *Pearls, Girls and Monty Bodkin*; and The Laurels, Burbage Road, of *Bachelors Anonymous*.

Incidentally, if you remember the denouement in *Sam the Sudden*, you will not be surprised to learn that Wodehouse's house and its neighbour had originally been one house, divided into two about ten years before his parents moved in.

Wodehouse knew his old house had been knocked down for re-development. He used its demolition as a sub-plot in *Company for Henry* and made his views clear in the introduction to the 1972 edition of *Sam the Sudden*.

> I did read somewhere about a firm of builders wanting to put up a block of flats in Croxted Road where I once lived in the first house on the left as you come up from the station. Gad, Sir, if anyone had tried to do that in my time,

I'd have horsewhipped them on the steps of their club, if they had a club.

Another old-fashioned signpost across the road points the way to West Norwood to the left and Dulwich Village and the Dulwich Picture Gallery to the right, and the No. 3 bus still halts on this corner as it did when Kay Derrick alighted from it in *Sam the Sudden*.

**3.** *Turn left and make your way down the left-hand side of Croxted Road. Keep walking until you reach Acacia Grove.*

Because of bomb damage in the war and subsequent redevelopment, all the houses and flats along here are new. In Wodehouse's day, the first turning on the left off Croxted Road was Acacia Grove, where Mike Jackson took lodgings in *Psmith in the City*. Until 1939, there was a small pond about ten yards north of the Acacia Grove corner, which Wodehouse made the home of the supercilious swans Egbert and Percy in *Big Money*.

About twenty yards past Acacia Grove, you will pass on your left three older houses, last of the Victorian dwellings that once lined Croxted Road. Wodehouse's old house, No. 62 up the road behind us, 'joined in indissoluble union' to No. 60, looked exactly like these. It was past pleasant houses like these with their small front gardens that Lord Biskerton walked when he came to collect the keys of Peacehaven, Mulberry Grove, from Mr Cornelius, the estate agent.

**4.** *At the junction of Croxted Road and Park Hall Road, turn left and follow the road around until you are opposite the Alleyn's Head on the other side of the road.*

The Alleyn's Head is a new building; the old pub, where Wodehouse used to have a beer and bread and cheese before watching the Dulwich Rugger team doing their stuff, stood on the side of the road where we are now, but it was bombed during the war.

> And his contentment deepened. For his eye, as he approached, was caught by what appeared to be a most admirable pub just round the corner. He went in and tested the beer. It was superb. Every explorer knows that the most important thing in a strange country is the locating of the drink supply: and the Biscuit, satisfied that this problem had been adequately solved, came out of the hostelry with a buoyant step, and a moment later the full beauties of Mulberry Grove were displayed before him.
>
> *(Big Money)*

Keep walking, and just before you reach the railway bridge, you come to Acacia Grove on the left.

### 5. *Acacia Grove – 'Mulberry Grove'*

To emphasise the intimacy of Mulberry Grove, Wodehouse drew it as much smaller than it is in real life. Walk up the left-hand side of Acacia Grove with the railway embankment on your right, and follow the street around, noting the footpath that runs away from you straight ahead up to the station alongside the embankment.

The footpath is a conclusive factor in the identification of Acacia Grove as Mulberry Grove. In *Big Money*, Lord Biskerton is about to take Kitchie Valentine to the pictures:

> And, while he knew that he was doing this merely because he was sorry for a lonely little girl, a stranger in a strange land, who had few pleasures, the last thing he wanted was a prominent member of the family dodging about the place, taking notes of his movements with bulging eyes.

He was therefore very uncomfortable when he found himself encumbered by the unexpected presence of his aunt, Lady Vera Mace. He was relieved to find she had to return to London and took swift action:

> "Well, I'll walk to the station with you."
> He hurried her round the corner and into the asphalt-paved, beehive-lined passage that led thither. Only

when they were out of sight of Mulberry Grove did his composure return.

Stay on the left-hand side of Acacia Grove and note a common feature of the houses here: the two small walls that run out from the front door. Many of them are empty, but No. 17, on the other side of the road, has two lions guarding the door while No. 7, on your left, has two stone balls fulfilling the same purpose. No. 6 has two more lions, while there are greyhounds outside Nos. 4 and 3.

At No. 2 are two sphinxes. It is very possible that other houses in Acacia Grove once had sphinxes guarding their doors, but these are the only ones left. You have arrived at the best candidate for the source of Peacehaven, Mulberry Grove, the residence of Lord Biskerton, of Stanhope Twine, of Freddie Widgeon and his cousin George.

> Peacehaven was a two-storey edifice in the Neo-Suburbo-Gothic style of architecture, constructed of bricks which appeared to be making a slow recovery from a recent attack of jaundice. Like so many of the houses in Valley Fields, it showed what Montgomery Perkins, the local architect could do when he set his mind to it. It was he, undoubtedly, who was responsible for the two stucco Sphinxes on either side of the steps leading to the front door.
>
> (*Big Money*, Chap. 5)

**6.** The rest of this walk looks at Wodehouse's memories of his time at Dulwich College rather than his stories of Valley Fields. In *Psmith in the City*, an unhappy Mike Jackson comes here, to 'Acacia Road, Dulwich' to look for lodgings. Like Wodehouse, Mike had been looking forward to going to university but family finances prevented it. Like Wodehouse, Mike had been found a berth in a bank, the New Asiatic, a thin disguise for the Hong Kong and Shanghai Bank that Wodehouse joined in the autumn of 1900.

At the end of Chapter 3, we are told that Mike left his lodgings in Acacia Road.

> A few steps took him to the railings that bounded the College grounds. It was late August, and the evenings had begun to close in. The cricket-field looked very cool and spacious in the dim light, with the school buildings looming vague and shadowy in the slight mist. The little gate by the railway bridge was not locked. He went in, and walked slowly across the turf towards the big clump of trees which marked the division between the cricket and football fields. . . . He sat down on a bench beside the second eleven telegraph board, and looked across the ground at the pavilion. For the first time that day he began to feel really homesick.

Knowing how important the College was in Wodehouse's life and how much he enjoyed his time here, I think it more than likely that, on an autumn evening in 1900, when he started work at the Bank, Wodehouse came back down here and did exactly what Mike Jackson did. It is something to think about as we retrace Mike's steps back down Acacia Grove.

### 7. Dulwich College
*Go back up Acacia Grove to Park Hall Road, turn left, and go under the railway bridge; cross the street to the black railings and gate around the school grounds. Walk up the road (Alleyn Park), with the college on your right.*

The gate just beyond the bridge into the school grounds is locked now, which means walking up Alleyn Park. The pavilion is on the right about fifty yards beyond the railings, and another hundred yards up Alleyn Park brings you level with the clump of trees Mike sat by. At the junction with Dulwich Common, turn right so the playing fields are still on your right. *(NOTE. If you are not visiting the College, return to West Dulwich Station by turning left at this corner and walking along Thurlow Park Road to the railway bridge.)*

**a.** Keep an eye on the large houses on the other side of the road. The third house you pass on your left, a cream-painted building with a balustrade along the roof, is Elm Lawn, Wodehouse's 'House' when he was a pupil here. If you remember the school stories, Wodehouse's schoolboys nearly all lived in Houses 'across the road' from the school in question. It was here, allegedly, that Wodehouse invented 'the po game'.

A long piece of string was lowered from an upstairs window at Elm Lawn, taken across the garden, and tied to another piece of string similarly lowered from the house next door, also a school House. Two china chamber pots, commonly called a 'po', were then suspended from the string though the handle, one at each end. So long as the string was taut, the pos would stay where they were, but letting out slack at one end of the string produced a satisfying crash and china debris all over the gardens below. That Wodehouse invented this pastime has never been proved, but it was firmly believed by many Old Alleynians, and it is also alleged that it needed very few instances to persuade the housemasters concerned to purchase durable chamber pots made of metal.

**b.** At the College entrance gate, turn right and go down to the main central block till you see the sign saying 'Reception'. Call in here for directions to the Wodehouse Library.

The main block remains as Wodehouse knew it over a century ago; he would still recognise the playing fields and even the houses around them. It is a pleasant spot to conclude our Wodehouse Walks.

*NOTE. The Wodehouse study with his desk and typewriter can usually be viewed without appointment during term-time. Applications for visits outside term-time should be made to Dulwich College, London SE21 7LD.*

# Appendix 1

# The Hybrid Walk and Omitted Stories

## A. The Hybrid Walk *(Map on page 98)*

This walk combines the first half of Walk 1 with all of Walk 2. I had suggested it to Norman a few years after *Three Wodehouse Walks* was published, for two reasons. First, The P G Wodehouse Society (UK) was then holding its thrice-yearly meetings at a pub just off the Strand, and Walk 2 ends at the Coal Hole on the Strand, making it more convenient for getting to meetings on time whenever Norman offered walks on the same day. But this meant that first-timers were missing out on Norman's classic walk.

Second, while the first part of Walk 1 is rich with Wodehouse sites, the second part (from the Burlington Arcade to the Sherlock Holmes Pub) is more focused on London, with only a few Wodehouse stories. Meanwhile, Walk 2 has quite a lot of Wodehouse from beginning to end. So the Hybrid Walk was born, and Norman agreed that it was a good idea (though be forewarned that it makes for a dashed long walk).

Taking the Hybrid Walk is a simple matter of veering off from the first walk either before or after going through the Burlington Arcade. The map on the next page shows the two routes you can take. Option 1 is to turn around before entering the Arcade, walk along Burlington Gardens into Vigo Street, then turn right on Regent Street and follow it all the way down to Piccadilly Circus. (If you choose to go this way, you might want to stop in front of 12 Burlington Gardens and read the story from the original Walk 1, below.)

Option 2 is to go through the Arcade. When you reach the exit onto Piccadilly, you would ordinarily turn right to continue Walk 1. Instead, turn left and follow the street down to Piccadilly Circus.

Once you reach Piccadilly Circus, either make your way across the roads to the point indicated on the map, or descend

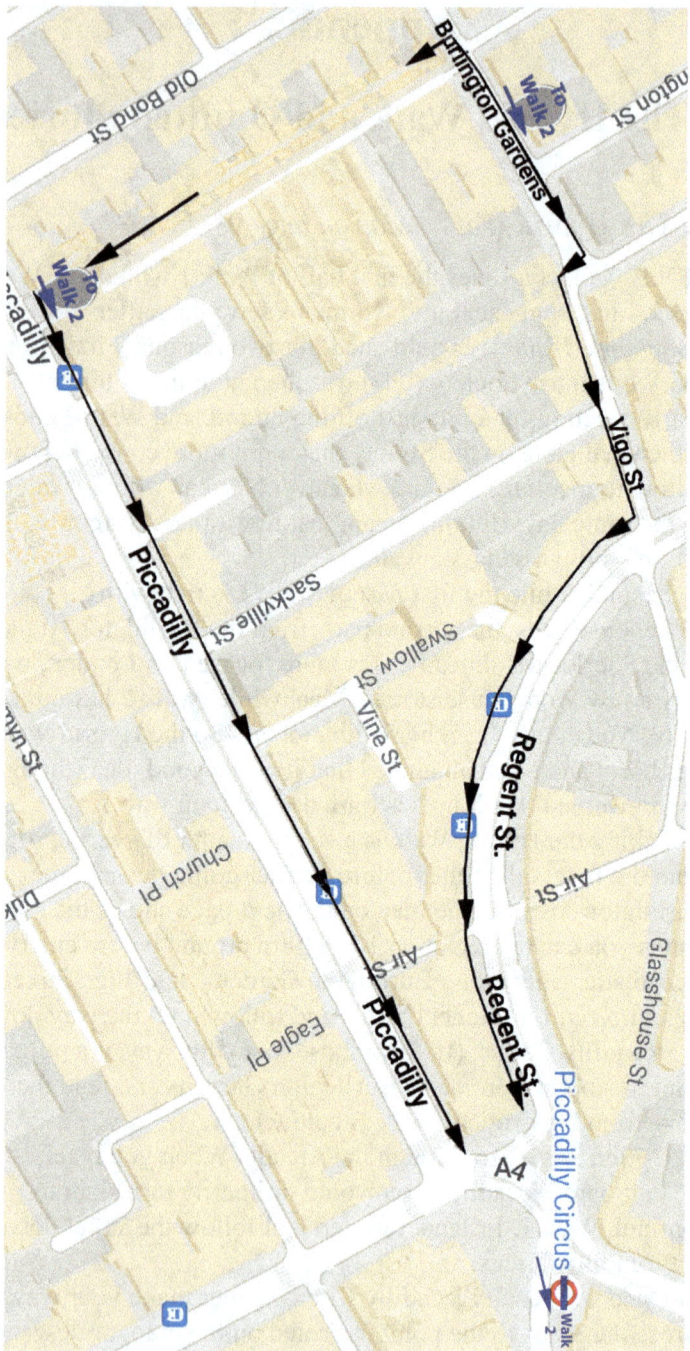

into the Underground station and then take the exit marked 'Subway 4', as described at the start of Walk 2. Have a spiffingly good walk!

## B. Omitted Stories from the First Edition

In preparing this revised edition of *Three Wodehouse Walks*, I had to deal with the disappearance of stores, pubs, or other sites that Norman talked about in the first edition. For most of these, I have altered the text where necessary, but here are two stories I had to leave out altogether.

### Walk 1

Norman's directions for stop number 13 in the first edition went like this: *Enter the Arcade and walk down it. About halfway down, there is a jewellery shop, Richard Ogden, on the right-hand side.* Having discovered that Richard Ogden Ltd had moved to 12 Burlington Gardens, only a few yards away from the Arcade, I considered tweaking the route in order to incorporate a stop there. However, since the story was a personal one for Norman and had nothing to do with either Wodehouse or London, I decided to eliminate it from the official walk.

But the story still deserves to be read. It was one of Norman's favourites – and one of mine, too, if only because he took such delight in telling it. I hope you enjoy it!

A personal story here but I make no apology for it. When my late wife Charlotte and I were preparing to get married back in 1961, the fashion among brides then was to have 24-carat gold wedding rings with ornate patterns on them. That was fine, but the washing powder we used in those days meant that the high-quality soft gold wore away very quickly and some brides we knew had to get new ones in a few years. Charlotte, being a good Scot, wasn't having that. She said she wanted a 9-carat gold ring; that is the lowest and hardest grade of gold as well as being the cheapest. I was horrified but she was adamant.

We went round the jewellers in Croydon where I lived then and they didn't want to know. The word 'cheapskate' was clearly what they had in mind, so I remembered that film *Breakfast at Tiffany's* – if you want service, go to the best – and we came up here to the Burlington Arcade to Richard Ogden's shop. We were very nervous as this tall man greeted us, Mr Ogden himself, and we very hesitantly explained what we wanted and why. He beamed at us: "How sensible! How practical! I wish my other customers were as farsighted as you, madam." He called for coffee for both of us, measured Charlotte's finger himself, produced a dozen 9-carat rings for her to choose from and generally made us feel like royalty.

Thirty years of happy marriage went by, and I asked Charlotte what she wanted for our anniversary. She decided she would like one of those Russian rings, three intertwined rings of different colours of gold, so, since I was coming down to London from Cumbria anyway, I made a note of her ring size, came down and charged in here again. A tall, elderly man got up from behind a desk and wished me "Good morning" and I was so surprised, I said exactly the wrong thing: "Good Lord, Mr Ogden, I thought you'd be dead by now!"

He smiled and said not quite yet, though he had retired but came into the shop occasionally. I told him how nervous we had been 30 years before, how kind he had been and explained I had come back to buy another ring. A smile spread across his face, and he called out: "Miss So-and-So! A cup of coffee for a regular customer!"

## Walk 2

This story had been included in stop 23 of the second walk and became obsolete almost as soon as *Three Wodehouse Walks* was published. More on that after Norman's story.

On the other side of the road from you, a few yards upstream is a small steamer, now a floating restaurant. It is called the *Queen Mary* – and it is the real, original *Queen Mary*. It is another example of the splendid mistakes that officialdom makes every so often. We saw how the Piazza in Covent Garden has been wrongly named for over three hundred years. Well, the bridge we have just walked under is Waterloo Bridge. When Parliament agreed a bridge should be built here, they named it as the Strand Bridge, built it as the Strand Bridge, and the Duke of Wellington opened it in 1817 as the Strand Bridge. But the opening ceremony took place on the second anniversary of Waterloo, so Londoners decided to call it Waterloo Bridge and continued to do so with such determination that Parliament had to pass an enabling Act to change the name. And Cleopatra's Needle, 100 yards further along the Embankment, has nothing whatsoever to do with Cleopatra. It was erected by the Pharaoh Thothmes III in 1450 BC but, long after her death, it was moved to the grounds of what had once been Cleopatra's palace. Londoners had never heard of Thothmes, but they had all heard of Cleopatra, so they decided to call it Cleopatra's Needle – and Cleopatra's Needle it remains today.

Now, back to the *Queen Mary*. The Cunard steamship line began in 1839, and their first four ships were the *Acadia*, *Britannia*, *Caledonia* and *Columbia*, starting the tradition of Cunard ships having names ending in the letters 'ia'. For nearly a hundred years, all their ships had names ending in 'ia'. So, in 1935 when the Atlantic liner route rivalry was at its height and they were building the biggest, fastest liner the world had ever seen, they decided to call it the *Victoria* – after Queen Victoria. But because Victoria had died only 34 years before, they reckoned they had better get permission and asked for an audience with King George V.

They got their audience and all trooped in, told the King they were building this super, new giant liner and would like his permission to name it after England's greatest Queen. Unfortunately, that is as far as they got. According to contemporary accounts, the King stopped them right there. He thoroughly approved; he thought it was a splendid idea – and then he added: "Mary will be delighted! I'll go and tell her now!" and vanished to do so. Consternation among the Cunard directors – followed by some very rapid re-painting on Clydebank – and an offer he couldn't refuse made to the owner of that small steamer over there. Under British shipping law, you cannot have two ships with the same name – so that small Clyde

steamer became, overnight, the *Queen Mary II*. And
Cunard had its first ship not ending with the letters 'ia'.
As I am sure you all know, she was the biggest and best
of the great liners, and once carried a complete American
army division of 16,000 men across the Atlantic during
the war unescorted, since she was the fastest ship afloat.
Sadly, she is now a floating hotel lying off Long Beach,
California. But, since her propellers have been taken out of
her, she now counts as a building – and that small floating
restaurant over there has now resumed her original name.
She is, once again, the one and only *Queen Mary*!

In case you are wondering, the *Victoria* was at last
launched in December 2007 – only 73 years late.

A great story, but there was a problem: in November 2009
the floating restaurant *Queen Mary* left her mooring beside
the Savoy Hotel and was towed across to France to become a
restaurant at La Rochelle (or so was our understanding of her
fate). Her place on the Thames was taken up by the Savoy Pier,
which was itself replaced by a mooring pontoon in 2020. The
*Queen Mary*'s absence was explained in an errata inserted into
*Three Wodehouse Walks*, which ended as follows:

*Some 250 feet long and 1,000 tons displacement, the*
*Queen Mary is one eightieth the size of her better-known*
*namesake. Another feature of London's landscape becomes*
*history.*

# Appendix 2

# Other Wodehouse Locations in London

This is a list of Wodehouse-related London locations not covered on Norman's walks (with one exception, 11 King Street). Descriptions in roman type are principally Norman's original text; *my insertions are in italics*. This was mostly adapted from the chapter 'London Locations' in *A Wodehouse Handbook*, Volume 1; I included some more from Norman's series 'Where Was Wodehouse? And When?' in September issues of *By The Way*, the occasional newsletter of The P G Wodehouse Society UK, and from notes he left behind. My deepest thanks to Robert Bruce and Richard Burnip for providing new or additional information on several of these sites. See Appendix 3 for information on a Wodehouse walk that Richard conducts for London Walks, and on how to get a map of Wodehouse locations throughout England, with descriptions written by Robert. –EWM

## A. Some of Wodehouse's Personal Addresses
*Note that in the 1920s and '30s, Wodehouse crisscrossed the Atlantic frequently, during which time he would take short-term leases on houses and flats in London. Only a few of those short-stay locations are included here. I have listed these addresses chronologically and included dates when PGW lived at each location.*

**Markham Square, Chelsea** (*1900*)  Wodehouse's first lodgings were in Markham Square, off King's Road, Chelsea. In *Not George Washington* he called it Manresa Road, which lies further to the west; I do not know why. Markham Square features in 'Ukridge's Accident Syndicate' – "a dismal backwater where he had once had rooms".

**22 (23) Walpole Street, Chelsea** (*1902–08*)  Wodehouse took lodgings here, in the last house on the left-hand side as you walk down from the King's Road. With a break for his sojourn down at Emsworth, this remained his London address till late 1908. I have seen many letters he wrote from here and was puzzled for a long time as to why the house number changed from No. 22 to 23 and back again. *Kelly's Directories* show that it was No. 23 in 1898, No. 24 in 1906 (there is no No. 22 listed), No. 22 in 1907 (there is no No. 23 listed), and in 1910 it reverted to No. 23 (but Nos. 21 and 22 had vanished). Perhaps the neighbouring houses were split, re-numbered as separate dwellings, and then restored by later owners? Certainly the Post Office took a very relaxed view of such re-numbering till the 1930s.

Wodehouse used this as the address of the main hero, Cloyster (based upon himself), in *Not George Washington*. Nearly twenty years later Denis Mackail lived in the same house, became famous when he wrote *Greenery Street* (based on Walpole Street), and was delighted to find Wodehouse had lived there before him. Mrs Maxtone-Graham, author of *Mrs Miniver*, took the house after the Mackails.

**124 Clement's Inn**, alongside the Law Courts in the Strand (*1908*) After Walpole Street, Wodehouse took lodgings here, as did Psmith and Mike Jackson in *Psmith in the City*. Clement's Inn has subsequently been rebuilt as solicitors' offices, though its front replicates the old façade.

**99/101 Ebury Street**, a lodging house kept by John Holborn (*1911*) Wodehouse's address here is from the 2/3 April 1911 Census; my thanks to Murray Hedgcock for this information. Corcoran, the narrator of *Ukridge,* has lodgings in Ebury St.

**3 Queen's Club Terrace. (now Queen's Club Gardens)** (*1913*) The January 1913 edition of the London Telephone Directory has PG at this address. My thanks again to Murray Hedgcock for this.

**94 Prince of Wales Mansions, Battersea** (*1913–14*) Wodehouse moved in with C.H. Bovill, an erstwhile colleague on *The Globe*. They collaborated on the unsuccessful stage sketch *Nuts and Wine* (1914), but achieved more success with their jointly written *A Man of Means* for the *Strand* magazine.

Their Battersea flat featured in 'The Romance of an Ugly Policeman' and in *Bill the Conqueror;* Jerry Vail lived there in *Pigs Have Wings*, and Leila York remembered it fondly in *Ice in the Bedroom*.

**16 Walton Street, South Kensington** (*1919–20*)  Three biographers believe the Wodehouses came over to London in 1918 and took this house to be near Leonora at school at Bromley, Kent. I believe this is incorrect for several reasons. From his letters, Wodehouse was certainly in America up to June and then again in September 1918. Also, as becomes clear in letters from 1921, Leonora did not move to the school in Bromley (south east of London) until 1921. Further, writing and rehearsing *The Girl Behind the Gun* occupied PG's time from July to its September opening. Finally, the war was still on and U-boats were attacking American ships. I do not think PG travelled to England in 1918.

There is an unofficial plaque on the house stating that PGW lived here 1918–1920. The only indication as to who put it there are the mysterious initials on it: 'L.L.A.D.' I have made strenuous efforts to trace these, but the best suggestion I have received so far is that they stand for 'Lord love a duck'!

**11 King Street, St James's** (*Flat 43, ca. late 1921–early 1922 plus sometime in 1923*)  *A lot of guesswork here: Wodehouse wrote from this address in December 1921; he and Ethel were at 18 Berkeley St by February 1922. They returned at some point since PG wrote from here in August 1923.)* Freddie Threepwood has a flat here in 'Lord Emsworth Acts for the Best' (*as noted in Walk 1*).

**4 Onslow Square, South Kensington** (*1922; following their stay at 18 Berkeley St, then a short trip to New York, the Wodehouses moved here for a few months.*)  This later became the residence of Mabel in 'A Bit of Luck for Mabel' and of Bunny Farringdon in *Cocktail Time*.

**23 Gilbert Street, Mayfair** (*1924–25*)  *The Wodehouses moved here in October 1924 and apparently used the house whenever they were in London. They retained the tenancy for app. seven months. In April 1925 Wodehouse gave this address on his proposal form for the Beefsteak Club.*

**The Manor, Davies Street, Mayfair** (*early 1926*)  In *Big Money*, Ann Moon stays here with Lady Vera Mace.

**17 Dunraven Street, Mayfair** (originally 17 Norfolk Street) (*1926–ca. 1938*)  The Wodehouses initially rented the house at 17 Norfolk Street. Ethel bought it two years later, and it became the London residence of Lord Emsworth in *Summer Lightning*. In 1938 the street was re-named Dunraven Street, and on 3 June 1988 Queen Elizabeth the Queen Mother unveiled the official blue plaque now to be seen on No. 17. It was a splendid occasion, and Her Majesty said afterwards she hoped I didn't mind her quoting me in her speech. I told her I didn't mind a bit.

*Note: English Heritage's website says the Wodehouses lived here between 1927 and 1934, but from PG's letters, it was definitely longer than that. PG and Ethel frequently let the house in the 1930s. The last mention of it in his letters is in June 1938. Thanks to Richard Burnip for pointing out that this is where Ronnie Fish introduces Sue Brown (calling her Myra Schoonmaker) to Lady Constance in* Summer Lightning.

**19 Grosvenor Hill, Mayfair** (*formerly Grosvenor Mews, 1931–32*)  The Wodehouses had let Norfolk Street, so they rented a flat at 19 Grosvenor Mews on their return from Hollywood in 1931. The following year they came back here on a short trip from their house in South of France. (This was the period when staying more than six months in England rendered Wodehouse liable to UK taxes.)

# B. Personal Addresses Used in PGW Books

*Wodehouse inserted addresses of people he knew into his books, both before and after he moved to the US in 1947. Here are just a few of them.*

**Bedford Row**. Wodehouse's UK literary agent A.P. Watt moved to No. 26 Bedford Row after the war. Wodehouse installed the solicitors Messrs Scrope, Ashby and Pemberton here in *The Girl in Blue*. In *Bachelors Anonymous*, Messrs. Nichols, Erridge, Trubshaw and Nichols are at No. 27.

**31 Chelsea Square**. In *The Girl in Blue*, this was the home of the lawyer Willoughby Scrope. When the book was written, it was also the address of another lawyer: Wodehouse's grandson, Edward Cazalet.

**Chesterfield Hill, Mayfair** (was John Street). Willoughby Braddock lived on John Street in *Sam the Sudden*. I find it no coincidence that 9 John Street, Mayfair, was the London residence of Wodehouse's friend Charles Le Strange. John Street is now named Chesterfield Hill. (*Note: Chesterfield Hill intersects with Hay's Mews, about which see Walk 1.*)

**Eaton Square**. Mentioned in several books up to 1930. The two late references in *Ice in the Bedroom* (Oofy Prosser) and *The Girl in Blue* (Dame Florence Faye) reflected the move here of Thelma Cazalet-Keir from Fountain Court (see below).

**Ennismore Gardens, Kensington**. The home of Muriel Branksome's aunt in 'The Voice from the Past', Wodehouse knew it as the London address of Mrs Susan Corbett, his neighbour in Shropshire, sister of Mrs Bowes-Lyon (see 22 Ovington Crescent, below). Forty years later, the house next door became the address of Wodehouse's granddaughter, Sheran Hornby, which is why 'Enniston Gardens' became the London residence of Ivor Llewellyn in *Bachelors Anonymous*.

**Fountain Court**. This smart block of flats in Park Lane, from 1954 to 1958 the residence of Thelma Cazalet-Keir, sister of Wodehouse's son-in-law, became the residence of Sally Fitch in *Bachelors Anonymous*. (*Richard Burnip wonders whether Wodehouse might have had Fountain Court in mind when, in*

'Jeeves and the Greasy Bird', Bertie implies that he now has a flat in Park Lane. Mere speculation, of course, but it's an idea I'm sure Norman would have seriously considered.)

**22 Ovington Crescent** was the home of Mrs Bowes-Lyon and her three daughters, whom Wodehouse had met in Stableford, Shropshire. He dedicated his first book to the three little girls. From 1902 to 1905, he used to go to tea with them on Sundays and make up Mrs Bowes-Lyon's numbers if she was a man short for dinner. His early notebooks are full of talk he heard at her table or memorable remarks by the three girls. He used 22 'Ovingdon' Square as Jill Mariner's address in *Jill the Reckless* (*The Little Warrior*).

**12 Thurloe Square, South Kensington**. Among the many relatives who kept an eye on young Pelham during his early days in London was his Aunt Julie of Thurloe Square, widow of his uncle Hugh Pollexfen Deane, a Colonial civil servant. It was probably the colonial widow connection that suggested Thurloe Square as the address for Lady Lakenheath of *Love Among the Chickens* and 'Ukridge Rounds a Nasty Corner' and of Mrs Winnington-Bates in *Sam the Sudden*.

**6 Wilbraham Place, Sloane Street**. I was surprised when Wodehouse gave this ultra-respectable address later to Mustard Pott in *Uncle Fred in the Springtime*. I wonder if it was a private joke? Did Wodehouse put him here to enjoy the incongruity of making him a neighbour of an ultra-respectable Wodehouse cousin, Major Sir Frederick Wodehouse KCB, KCVO, Deputy Commissioner City of London Police, who lived at 9 Wilbraham Mansions, Wilbraham Place, from 1900 to 1918?

## C. Other Notable London Locations

*This includes some well-known London sites, fictional locations for which Norman had determined a real-life equivalent, and sites with which Wodehouse was associated in some way.*

**Albany, Piccadilly** (*Albany Court Yard, across from Hatchards bookstore*) William Bates ('The Man Upstairs') and Freddie Rooke of *Jill the Reckless* lived here. The Albany, built when America was still a colony, remains a smart, expensive address in London for bachelors who want rooms in the centre of town.

*Richard Burnhip adds:* We meet Sir Godfrey Tanner (and the faithful Jevons) here at the start of 'Creatures of Impulse'. And Wodehouse makes a number of references to Raffles, who also lived here.

**The Berkeley Hotel, Wilton Place** (formerly Piccadilly). Popular for lunch among the younger smart set in the 1920s, the Berkeley had a maître d'hôtel, Ferraro, who was famous for the strict control he exercised (see *A Wodehouse Handbook*, Volume 2). Mentioned in four Wodehouse books, the hotel has moved from Piccadilly to Wilton Place.

**Berkeley Mansions**, the block of flats at the northwest corner of Berkeley Square, appeared as Bertie's address in *Thank You, Jeeves*; *Right Ho, Jeeves*; and later. Gally Threepwood lived there in *A Pelican at Blandings*. PGW never brought them together, but Bertie certainly knew about Blandings and Gally knew about Jeeves. Perhaps they exchanged gossip when they met on the stairs.

*Note: Norman had also written: "Berkeley Mansions was demolished in late 2002", which is not quite correct. Richard Burnip sets the record straight:* Berkeley Mansions was at 1 Mount Street. The actual entrance was on the corner of Mount and Davies Streets, so Bertie could walk straight across the road into Berkeley Square. It was more or less in the northwest corner of Berkeley Square, so I've always assumed it must be the one Norman wrote about. Nos 1–3 have been rebuilt, but 4 and 5 survive, and 5 was a mirror image of no. 1. *(See photo on next page.)*

*Berkeley Square, as seen in an early postcard. The entrance to Berkeley Mansions (whose address was 1 Mount Street) can be seen above the '01'. (Photo courtesy of Richard Burnip)*

**Berkeley Square, Mayfair**. This Square was home to a series of characters, including the Earl of Biddlecombe ('Came the Dawn'), Earl of Blotsam ('The Knightly Quest of Mervyn'), and Lady Punter in 'The Amazing Hat Mystery'. No. 46 Berkeley Square was the home of Lord Mildmay, the steeplechase rider whom Wodehouse came to know when Leonora married Mildmay's racing partner, Peter Cazalet. *Richard Burnip gives us more ripe stuff:* Bertie admired Rosie M. Banks: "So far as looks went, she might have stepped straight out of Berkeley Square." Wodehouse would certainly have seen the numerous court dressmakers and milliners around the square in the 1920s and '30s.

**Bertie's bookstore**. *Remember when Bertie tries to purchase a copy of Spinoza's latest and ends up with Florence Craye's* Spindrift *instead? My thanks to Richard Burnip for pointing out the likeliest candidates for the book shop: Sotheran's (est. 1791), which has been at 2–5 Sackville Street, off Piccadilly, since 1815; or Hatchards, a fixture at 187 Piccadilly since 1797. Both bookstores are well worth visiting, and – who knows? – there may be a* Spindrift *or two left in stock.*

110

**235 Brompton Road**. The antique shop PGW referred to "in the Brompton Road – it's just past the Oratory" bears an astonishing resemblance to James Hardy & Co, 235 Brompton Road (their letterhead says 'Opposite the Oratory'), who are still flourishing on the site. I do not claim that it is Hardy's but would point out it was the only jeweller and silversmith within a quarter of a mile when PGW wrote about it. I couldn't afford to buy a cow creamer there, so I just bought a small silver pig instead. It seemed appropriate.

**Bruton Street**. *In* The Girl on the Boat, *the Marlowes' family home is on Bruton Street. Ian Hay had lived at 21 Bruton Street before moving to 47 Charles Street (the address PGW gave to Aunt Dahlia; see Walk 1).*

**Claridge's**. Mentioned in seven books from *The Inimitable Jeeves* to *Cocktail Time*, Claridges's stands at the corner of Brook Street and Davies Street. (*Note: Norman always maintained that Claridge's was the original of Wodehouse's Barribault Hotel. For more on this, see* A Wodehouse Handbook, *Volume 1, Chapter 25.*)

**The Gaiety Theatre and Aldwyich Theatre**. *My thanks to Robert Bruce for reminding me that Wodehouse was resident lyricist at these two theatres from 1906. The Gaiety, mentioned in Walk 2, stood at 1 Aldwych – that is, the corner of Aldwych and the Strand – and was, as Robert tells us, "the biggest musical theatre of its time". Two plaques mark the spot where the two Gaiety buildings once stood. While the Gaiety is long gone, the Aldwych is still in situ at 49 Aldwych. (Photo to the right courtesy of Robert)*

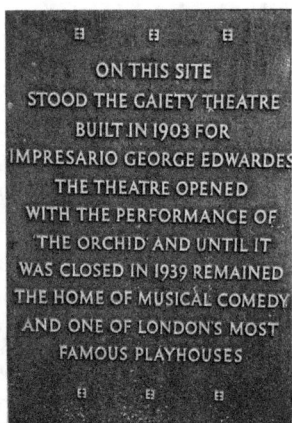

ON THIS SITE
STOOD THE GAIETY THEATRE
BUILT IN 1903 FOR
IMPRESARIO GEORGE EDWARDES
THE THEATRE OPENED
WITH THE PERFORMANCE OF
'THE ORCHID' AND UNTIL IT
WAS CLOSED IN 1939 REMAINED
THE HOME OF MUSICAL COMEDY
AND ONE OF LONDON'S MOST
FAMOUS PLAYHOUSES

**Grosvenor Square, Mayfair**. Grosvenor Square was given as the address of several characters in Wodehouse's novels. The Cazalet family, into which Leonora married, had their London residence at 66 Grosvenor Street, just off the Square.

**Hong Kong and Shangkai Bank**, 41 Lombard Street. *The bank where Wodehouse worked after leaving Dulwich College in 1900 – and which clearly was the model for the London and Oriental Bank (*Mike*) and New Asiatic Bank (*Psmith in the City *and others) – is no longer here. However, as Robert Bruce points out, "the building opposite gives a good idea of how the premises looked".*

**Hotel Magnificent**. This hotel stood opposite the Senior Conservative Club in 'The Custody of the Pumpkin'. It is not difficult to identify it as the Hotel Victoria, which stood across Northumberland Avenue from the Constitutional Club (see Walk 1). Wodehouse used to get his hair cut here, which is why, in *Hot Water*, Packy Franklyn cut Senator Opal's hair in the 'Hotel Northumberland' on the same site. The building is still there but is now part of the London School of Economics.

*Richard Burnip adds:* I wonder if the 'Hotel Northumberland' was another of Wodehouse's deliberate references to Sherlock Holmes – in this instance the 'Northumberland Hotel' in *The Hound of the Baskervilles*, which was certainly nearby and may have been based on the Victoria Hotel.

**The Junior Lipstick** club in 'Came the Dawn' is situated where "Seamore Place to the west meets Charles Street to the east". A street directory of the time shows that can only be the Curzon House Club (for ladies) where Leonora was a member. (Seamore Place became part of Curzon Street in 1938.)

*Richard Burnip fills in the gaps:* The Curzon House Club was in Curzon House at the corner of Curzon Street and Derby Street. Curzon House was created out of three 18th century houses in the 1880s, which is why it has the address 21–23 Curzon Street (although this is not always given in the street directories). With Seamore Place a block along to the west and Charles Street a little further off to the north-east, it certainly fits the description. As far as I know, it ceased to be a club for ladies in the early 1960s and was a casino for a number of years. At various times the adjoining house, number 20, was also listed as part of the club. Happily, both buildings are still there.

**Murphy's Mews**, the address of the unpleasant Jaklyn Warner in *Bachelors Anonymous*. There is not nor ever has been a Murphy's Mews in London. Because Wodehouse had left England well over thirty years before, he had forgotten the names of the small back streets of Chelsea and Pimlico he had known as a young man. I only include it because it was while he was writing the book that I managed to find and send him the one Pink 'Un and Pelican book he did not have – and he was very grateful. Probably pure coincidence, but I am very proud of it.

**Park Street, Mayfair**. No. 26 Park Street had been the home of Lord Wodehouse (heir to the Earl of Kimberley), whom P.G. Wodehouse knew. No. 36A Park Street was the residence of Aurelia Cammarleigh in 'The Reverent Wooing of Archibald' and 'Archibald and the Masses'.

**Tilbury House/Mammoth Publishing Company**. The original of Tilbury House (aka Mammoth Publishing Company), Lord Northcliffe's Carmelite House at 8 Carmelite Street, is still very much as PGW described. Built around the 1870s, it is a fine example of the red-brick Gothic revival office buildings popular at the time. Chimp Twist's office was on the north side of Tallis Street, which intersects with Carmelite Street.

*Robert Bruce writes:* Follow the instructions in the opening sentence of *Heavy Weather*, and you will find yourself walking down Carmelite Street." Carmelite House, where Bingo Little edited *Wee Tots* and Monty Bodkin was sacked after spicing up *Tiny Tots*, will be on your right.

**Washington Hotel, Curzon Street**. This was the Lincoln Hotel in *Money for Nothing*. Why Wodehouse changed the name of the real Washington Hotel, where he spent a few days while writing the book in 1926, is beyond me. But at least he kept it American.

**Westminster Abbey**. *In September 2019, a memorial stone to P. G. Wodehouse was unveiled and dedicated here – a long overdue honour. This was the result of The P G Wodehouse*

*Society (UK)'s successful effort to have PGW included among the pantheon of literary greats memorialised in the Abbey. Wodehouse's stone (seen below) is located in the South Quire Aisle, near Poet's Corner.*

## D. Wimbledon Common

Some miles southwest of central London is a beautiful stretch of open heath land known as Wimbledon Common. For more than a century, the houses along Parkside, the road running down the eastern side of the Common, have symbolised wealth and respectability. In *Ukridge,* Miss Julia Ukridge lives at Heath House; in *Bill the Conqueror*, Flick Sheridan lives in a house of the same name. In 'Success Story', Ukridge turns The Cedars, Wimbledon Common, into a gambling hell; in 'Bingo and the Peke Crisis', Bingo and Mrs Bingo Little live there. The houses along Parkside appear in *The Mating Season, Nothing Serious, A Few Quick Ones* and *Frozen Assets*.

Wodehouse came to know Parkside around 1900–05 when his cousin Edward Isaac used to take him down to tea with an Isaac aunt, the extremely dignified widow of a judge. Her house, Gayton Lodge, which fitted every description Wodehouse gave us, has been replaced by the Albemarle Apartments, one of the blocks of flats which now occupy much of Parkside. However, a survivor of the impressive mansions that once lined the road can be seen at 49 Parkside (Dominion

House), once the home of Jenny Lind. A single glance shows the accuracy of Wodehouse's description of Lord Tilbury's house in *Frozen Assets*.

Lauriston Road runs off the south side of Wimbledon Common. At the corner of Lauriston Road and The Ridgeway is The Red House, where Perceval Graves brought Wodehouse to meet his family in 1901/2. Wodehouse became friends with them and wrote prefaces for some of Charles Graves' books. Graves's younger brother Robert, the poet, recalled that Wodehouse once gave him twopence to buy sweets, in return for which gesture Robert felt he could never criticize Wodehouse's writing. By a happy coincidence, the late Patrick Wodehouse (PGW's nephew) lived less than fifty yards away till his death in 2011.

(From *A Wodehouse Handbook*, Volume 1, Chapter 7)

# Appendix 3

## Further Resources

### *Blandings and Beyond: PG Wodehouse's England*

Herb Lester Associates is a company specialising in travel-related guides and other products, including maps centring on England's cultural heritage. Early in 2023, Robert Bruce suggested to them that they really ought to have a map showing the key sites in Wodehouse's England – and before he knew it, he was writing it, basing a lot of his text on Norman's work. The map was published in October 2023, and it is a corker – well illustrated and tremendously informative, a perfect guide for fans of Wodehouse. (One small caveat: due to an error in the original edition of *Three Wodehouse Walks*, the map gives 15 Berkeley Street as Bertie Wooster's address. It is actually 18 Berkeley Street (see Walk 1).)

*Blandings and Beyond* can be purchased directly from Herb Lester Associates at herblester.com. In November 2023, the price was £12 in the UK and $16 in the US.

## *What Ho, Jeeves! – The London of P.G. Wodehouse*

For many years actor, writer, and historian Richard Burnip has conducted walks for the organization London Walks. This includes one with the above title that he conducts both in person and virtually (via Zoom). In January 2010, Norman, Hilary & Robert Bruce, and I signed up for Richard's walk on an incognito basis and enjoyed it thoroughly – it is the goods! You can read about that day in *Wooster Sauce*, March 2010, page 11. I've been recommending this walk ever since.

Richard's walk covers a mostly different section of Mayfair, so there is only a bit of overlap with Norman's Walk 1. Enjoyment of the experience is enhanced by the number of Wodehouse quotes that Richard disperses liberally throughout his presentation. The fee as of 2023 is £15 for adults, £10 for seniors and students, and £5 for children 8–15 accompanied by their parents. To find out when the next walk will be, either in London or online, go to the London Walks website (www. walks.com/) and search for 'Wodehouse'. If your interests range beyond Wodehouse, be sure to check out all the other walks on offer – they are well worth the price.

---

# *The P G Wodehouse Society (UK)*
### www.pgwodehousesociety.org.uk

The P G Wodehouse Society (UK) was formed in 1997 to promote the enjoyment of the writings of the twentieth century's greatest humorist. The Society publishes a quarterly magazine, *Wooster Sauce*, which includes articles, features, reviews, and current Society news. Occasional special papers are also published. Society events include regular meetings in central London, cricket matches, and a formal biennial dinner, along with other activities.

### MEMBERSHIP ENQUIRIES

Membership of the Society is open to applicants from all parts of the world. As of 2023, the cost of a year's membership is £22. Enquiries and requests for membership forms should be made to info@pgwodehousesociety.org.uk.